Smile I
Ein Arbeitsbuch
für Unterricht und Selbststudium
19. Auflage

Mit Bescheid des Bundesministeriums für Unterricht und kulturelle Angelegenheiten vom 7. Juli 1998, GZ 47.225/1-III/D/13/98 gemäß § 14 Absatz 2 und 5 des Schulunterrichtsgesetzes BGBl. Nr. 472/86 und gemäß den derzeit geltenden Lehrplänen als für den Unterrichtsgebrauch an Hauptschulen und an allgemein bildenden höheren Schulen für die 1. Klasse im Unterrichtsgegenstand Englisch geeignet erklärt.

Schulbuch Nummer 8536

Umwelthinweis: Gedruckt auf chlorfrei gebleichtem Papier.

Ernst Denkmayr GmbH
Verlag und Druck
Katsdorf - Linz - Wels - Wien
Printed in Austria

ISBN 3-901838-17-1
W 1206

Liebe Schülerin, lieber Schüler !

In meiner langjährigen Unterrichtstätigkeit habe ich die Erfahrung gemacht, dass Übungsbeispiele zusätzlich zu Unterricht und Schulbüchern unentbehrlich sind.
Dieses Übungsbuch soll dir helfen, deine Grammatikkenntnisse zu vertiefen. Dadurch wirst du an Sicherheit im Umgang mit der englischen Sprache gewinnen.

Zu Beginn jedes Kapitels findest du eine übersichtliche Zusammenstellung der Regeln, anschließend viele Übungsbeispiele.
Wenn dir ein Vokabel unbekannt ist, kannst du im "Words"-Teil die deutsche Übersetzung finden.
Da dir sicher nur einzelne englische Vornamen geläufig sind, habe ich anschließend einige häufig vorkommende Namen nach Geschlecht geordnet zusammengestellt.
Mit dem "Key" am Ende des Buches kannst du leicht überprüfen, ob du fehlerfrei gearbeitet hast.

Ich wünsche dir recht viel Freude beim Üben!

Prof.Mag.Claudia Lichtenwagner

CONTENTS

page

Singular and plural 1
Indefinite article 1
Personal pronouns 6
The verb *to be* 6
Personal pronouns and possessive adjectives 11
Have (got) and *has (got)* 18
The verb 20
Questions 24
Mixed exercises: *have-has,verb,article,question* 28
They're - there - their 29
Its or *it's* 30
What do you say when.... 31
Command 32
Translate 33
Negation 34
Plural 38
Short forms 42
Personal pronouns object form 44
Present tense simple form 50
Present tense progressive form 51
Exercises: simple or progressive form 53
How to ask questions 59
Uncountable words 65
A - an - some 66
The possessive case 68
This - these, that - those 70
Word order 73
Past tense 76
List of irregular verbs 78
Present tense or past tense 79
Past tense questions 80
Going to future 82
Present simple, progressive, going to future, past tense 83
Questions: present tense, past tense, going to future 85
Words 86
List of girls' and boys' names 92
Key 93

SINGULAR AND PLURAL

Singular	Plural
one star	two star**s**
one ring	two ring**s**
a chair	four chair**s**
a dog	three dog**s**
a book	two book**s**
a desk	twenty desk**s**
a game	five game**s**
one door	three door**s**
an apple	two apple**s**
an orange	four orang**es** pron: [iz]

INDEFINITE ARTICLE

a / an

a banana	**an o**range
a sandwich	**an a**pple
a hamburger	**an i**ce cream
a snack	**an e**xercise book
a book	**an E**nglish name
a shirt	**an u**mbrella
a lolly	**an e**ar
a toffee	**an e**gg
a hot dog	**an e**ye
a sweet	**an i**sland
a chewing gum	**an u**gly monster

Attention !!!

a uniform	pron: [ju]	**an hour**	pron : [au]
a unit	pron: [ju]		
a university	pron: [ju]		

A OR AN

1. I want .... ice cream, please.
2. Is Ken .... name for ... boy or .... girl ?
3. I need .... exercise book and ..... good pen.
4. Give me .... rubber, please.
5. Sheila is .... English name.
6. Tim is ..... very good boy.
7. I need .... English book.
8. You need ..... new English book.
9. 'Top Ten' is ..... radio programme.
10. Do you want .... orange ? Yes, please !
11. Have you got .... brother ?
12. I have .... orange cat.
13. I have got .... blue pencil case.
14. There is .... exercise book on the desk.
15. Do you want ..... apple ?
16. You have got .... old schoolbag.
17. She is ..... old teacher.
18. He has ...... English car.
19. Josef is ..... Austrian boy.
20. Bill is .... English boy.
21. Judy is .... American girl.
22. I like .... orange for breakfast.
23. There is .... handbag on the chair.
24. This is .... old T-shirt.
25. Is he ..... English boy ? No, he is ..... Austrian boy.
26. Can I have ..... apple, please ?
27. Do you want .... ice cream ? Yes, please.
28. Do you want .... hamburger ? Yes, please.
29. Do you want ...... boiled egg for breakfast ? .... egg ?- No, thanks.
30. Have you got .... orange pullover ?
31. I have ..... cheese sandwich for breakfast.
32. I have ..... empty glass.
33. There is .... atlas on the floor.
34. I have got .... aunt in America.
35. Have you got ..... English book ? Yes, I have.
36. Frank is .... American boy.
37. Do you want .... lolly ? Yes, please.
38. Do you like .... pink felt-tip ?
39. I have got .... blue satchel and .... brown pencil case.

40. Have you got .... umbrella ? Yes, ... orange umbrella !
41. I have got ..... blue umbrella.
42. Robert, have you got .... earring ?
43. Do you like ... banana ?
44. We like ...... good breakfast.
45. Bill and Bob have got .... animal.
46. Bill and Bob have got ..... nice animal.
47. They wear .... nice uniform.
48. I have got .... uncle in England.
49. I do .... easy exercise.
50. I have ...... orange and ..... banana for breakfast.
51. Do you want ..... hamburger or ..... hot dog ?
52. You have got ...... nice pet.
53. This is .... expensive car.
54. There is .... hat on the chair.
55. I`ve got ..... good idea !
56. My cat is ..... nice animal.
57. Do you want .... lolly ?
58. .... orange floor is ugly.
59. Let`s have .... party !
60. .... party ! What .... great idea !
61. The band has .... new song.
62. I eat ... big orange.
63. Do you want .... orange ?
64. You have .... new T-shirt.
65. There is .... book on the desk.
66. Peter has got .... grey cat.
67. I have got .... headache.
68. We go to ..... snack bar.
69. I order .... hot dog.
70. You order .... hamburger.
71. I take ..... bite of the hamburger.
72. ...... lolly, please and ..... chewing gum.
73. On the table there is .... orange, ... apple and ...... glass of milk.
74. In Frank`s schoolbag there is ..... sharpener, ... biro, ... green apple.
75. In Bob`s schoolbag there is ..... fruit gum, ... lolly, ... exercise book.
76. In my schoolbag there is .... orange pen , ... blue rubber, ... felt pen.
77. In the classroom there is ... blue door and ..... green board.
78. In our class there is ..... overhead projector and ..... cassette recorder.
79. In the picture I see ...... boy, ... red car and ...... orange ball.
80. I have got .... black cap, ... orange blouse and ...... green shirt.

A OR AN

1. Do you want .... cup of tea ?
2. They live in ..... old house.
3. ..... mouse is ...... animal.
4. I am reading ...... interesting book now.
5. Can you give me ..... example ?
6. I don`t wear ..... uniform.
7. I buy .... hat and .... umbrella.
8. What .... ugly colour !
9. Please, come back in .... hour.
10. Austria is .... European country.
11. Ried hasn`t got ...... university.
12. He is .... dentist.
13. This is ..... old book.
14. We don`t have .... airport here.
15. Father has ..... accident.
16. Uncle Jim had ..... bad accident.
17. This is ...... very important question.
18. This is ..... important word.
19. Barbara works in .... office.
20. This is .... American word.
21. Please, buy me ..... earring.
22. Do you like .... hamburger ? No, I prefer .... orange.
23. I`d like to have .... apple, please.
24. I need ..... new car. I`ve got .... old one.
25. No, I don`t like .... orange hat.
26. I`ve got .... idea !! Let`s have .... party !
27. I need ..... new umbrella.
28. I`ve got .... very good idea ! Let`s buy .... apple-pie !
29. Could you please buy .... bottle of milk ?
30. They want to build .... airport near the park ! What .... idea !!!
31. This is .... expensive hotel.
32. ...... man is walking down the street.
33. Sally is ..... unhappy girl.
34. I have got .... aunt in France.
35. This is ...... useful present.
36. I want to spend my holidays on ..... island.

37. Look ! Bob has got .... red ear !
38. Britain is .... island.
39. Josef is .... Austrian schoolboy.
40. Sandy is ..... English schoolboy.
41. This is .... old locker.
42. No, ... orange jacket does not go with my red blouse.
43. We live in .... old house near the station.
44. This is .... expensive bike.
45. What`s that ? - That`s .... ordinary cake.
46. I must take .... exam next week.
47. She is .... arrogant girl.
48. Peter has .... empty glass.
49. This is ..... good story.
50. I want .... apple, ... green apple, please.
51. I like ..... roll for breakfast.
52. Austria is .... beautiful country.
53. We have got ..... new teacher.
54. Mrs Biggs is ..... nice teacher.
55. Ami is ..... funny clown.
56. This is ..... long telephone number.
57. I know ..... interesting story.
58. This is ..... interesting book.
59. In my room there is .... heavy locker.
60. I hear ..... awful noise.
61. Yummy, what .... tasty pizza !
62. What .... expensive mountain bike !
63. I have ..... new camera.
64. We have .... English breakfast.
65. I want ..... roll, ... glass of milk and ..... egg for breakfast.
66. Nigel is ..... superstar.
67. Pit has got ..... orange skateboard.
68. He sings .... awful song.
69. There is ..... overhead projector on the desk.
70. We have got ...... new English book.
71. This is .... English Christmas card.
72. Mr Miller has .... old castle.
73. Let`s have ..... ice cream !
74. What .... beautiful ring !
75. I take ... bite of the hot dog.
76. I pay for ...... hamburger and ..... orange juice.

PERSONAL PRONOUNS and THE VERB "TO BE"

I	am	Bill.
You	are	Cathy.
He	is	Tim.
She	is	Sue.
It	is	a cat.
We	are	hungry.
You	are	great!
They	are	super!

IS AM ARE

1. What .... your name ?
2. Sally, how .... you today ? I .... fine, thanks !
3. We .... sixteen girls in our class.
4. What colour .... your pullover, Pat ? It .... green.
5. I think your biro .... green.
6. What .... 'Tisch' in English ?
7. I think you .... right.
8. The children .... in the shop.
9. What colour .... your pen ?
10. What colour .... your books ?
11. Where .... the duster ?
12. Sandy, ... you a girl or a boy ?
13. What .... the time ? It .... ten o`clock.
14. .... you ready ? No, I .... not.
15. Where .... my pen ? It .... not in the pencil case.
16. Can I have a lolly ? Yes, here you ....
17. I think your chairs .... too small.
18. That .... very easy for me.
19. .... your socks green ? No, they .... blue.
20. That .... wrong.
21. Mum, this .... Jenny.- Hello Jenny !
22. .... your teachers nice ? Yes, they ....
23. My books .... on the desk.
24. This .... a nice cat.
25. What colour .... your curtains ?
26. Bob .... not at home.
27. I .... your new English teacher.
28. How much .... the pullover ? It .... sixty pounds.
29. How much .... the jeans ? They .... eighty pounds.
30. How many children .... there in this room ?
31. Where .... Bob and Bill ? They .... in the classroom.
32. Joe, ... this your new bike ? Yes, it .... !
33. Michael and Fred .... in one class. They .... clever.
34. We .... late for school.
35. My sister and I .... hungry.
36. Phil .... my best friend.
37. She .... a very nice girl.
38. .... there a mouse under the chair ?
39. Where .... Frank`s glasses ?

40. .... you Sandy`s sister ? - No, I .... not.
41. English .... very easy.
42. This .... my hamster.
43. Dad, this .... my friend Bill !
44. How many pencils .... there in your pencil case ?
45. You .... very nice.
46. How old .... you, Liz ?
47. What colour .... your trousers ?
48. How much .... your new pullover ?
49. .... you happy or .... you sad ?
50. I .... ready !
51. Where .... my socks ?
52. How .... you today ? Fine, thanks !
53. Mum, this .... Bill ! - Hello Bill !
54. You .... clever, Ben.
55. The mouse .... grey.
56. The T- shirt .... nice.
57. Where .... my English books ?
58. Pit .... in the classroom.
59. What colour .... your felt-pen ?
60. .... you hungry ? No, I .... not.
61. The children .... at school.
62. .... Sally sleepy ? Yes, she ....
63. The film .... great fun.
64. Mum and Dad .... not in the house.
65. Sandy .... shopping in town.
66. Your rubber .... in the schoolbag, but your books .... not.
67. We .... ready. Let`s go to Lisa.
68. They .... late for school.
69. .... this hat thirty pounds ? - Yes, it ....
70. .... the shoes pink ? - Yes, they ....
71. .... the new car expensive ? - Yes, it ....
72. Molly .... on her way home from school.
73. Sorry, I .... late.
74. The pudding .... lovely.
75. The boys .... in the playground.
76. The book .... easy to read.
77. .... the jeans expensive ? - Yes, they ....
78. .... the tights blue ? No, they .... not.
79. What colour .... the new curtains in the classroom ?
80. .... you Ben ? - No, I .... Bill.
81. They .... new at school. They .... nice children.

IS AM ARE

1. This ..... a blue schoolbag.
2. .... you Bob ?
3. What make ..... your car ?
4. Sue, how ..... you today ?
5. Where ...... my shoes ?
6. We ..... eleven girls in our class.
7. What colour ......your schoolbag, Bill ?
8. I .... a schoolboy.
9. They .... at school now.
10. I think your biro ...... green.
11. We ...... in the classroom.
12. These ...... his books.
13. .... she tired ?
14. What ..... ' Filzstift' in English ?
15. ..... he a good boy ?
16. What colour ...... your sharpener ?
17. ...... he right ?
18. It .... a nice dog.
19. How old ..... you ?
20. I think you ..... hungry.
21. The children ..... in the shop.
22. What colour .... Sandy's rubber ?
23. It ..... blue.
24. Where ..... the key ?
25. Pat, ... you a girl ? No, I ..... a boy !
26. ...... you ready ? Yes, I .... !
27. Where ..... my rubber ?
28. Can I have a lolly ? Yes, here you ..... !
29. The chairs ..... too small.
30. That .... easy for Ben !
31. What colour ..... your books ?
32. This .... Jim. He .... very nice.
33. My exercise books .... on the desk.
34. ..... you happy ? No, I ..... sad.
35. How ..... you today ? I ..... not so fine.
36. That .... right.
37. This ..... my sharpener.
38. She .... Sue.
39. It ..... the beginning of the schoolyear.
40. I ..... Tony.

41. They ..... ready.
42. Breakfast ..... ready !
43. 'The Hit Parade' ...... a radio programme.
44. Pam .... an English name.
45. What .... your name ?
46. You .... clever, William !
47. The cat ..... in the garden.
48. Mary's pencilcase ..... brown.
49. The mouse .... under the chair.
50. Take my hamburger. Here you ....
51. Mick .... in bed.
52. The garden .... full of flowers.
53. We .... not tired.
54. Ice cream .... super.
55. .... you Sally Roberts ? - No, I .... sorry, I .... Mandy Smith.
56. It .... cold in here.
57. Nigel .... tall. I .... small.
58. .... you alright, Ben ? - Yes, I ....
59. It .... a great birthday party.
60. .... he OK ? - Yes, he ....
61. The film .... super !
62. .... the glass empty ?
63. This shirt .... too big .
64. His trousers .... super !
65. How much .... the blue jeans ? - They .... sixty pounds.
66. The cat .... in front of the cupboard.
67. Where .... the children ? - They .... at school.
68. How much .... the green and blue trainers? - They .... fifty pounds.
69. How much .... three plus four ? - Three plus four .... seven.
70. How much .... ninety minus twenty ? - It .... seventy.
71. Where .... the blouse ? - It .... on the chair.
72. Peter .... at Sally`s party.
73. My coat .... in the locker.
74. Take the hot dog. It .... tasty.
75. Pat .... hungry.
76. The book on Jack`s desk .... green.
77. Where .... Pam ? She .... in bed.
78. Excuse me, how much .... the socks ?
79. I .... ten years old. Pit .... eleven.
80. John and I .... brother and sister.
81. Jimmy .... a very nice boy.
82. The shoes .... seventy pounds. That .... expensive !

PERSONAL PRONOUNS **POSSESSIVE ADJECTIVES**

I	like	**my**	cat.
You	love	**your**	dog.
He	feeds	**his**	fish.
She	plays with	**her**	doll.
It	likes	**its**	bone.
We	look at	**our**	dog.
You	love	**your**	mice.
They	help	**their**	cat.

PERSONAL PRONOUNS and POSSESSIVE ADJECTIVES

Dear Billy,
Thank........ for .... letter ! How are ..... ? .... am fine !
...... send ...... a photo of .... class. .... all wear school uniforms.
.... look nice in .... uniforms ! .... uniforms are super: blue trousers, a blue pullover, a white shirt and ..... ties are red.
Do .... like the photo ?
Have ..... got a brother or a sister ? .... brother is eleven years old.
.... have got a sister, too. .... name is Sarah. .... is lovely and ...... like Sarah very much. .... play very much and ...... have a lot of fun.
Do .... have a photo of .... school or .... house and .... family ?
Have .... got a pet ? .... have a cat.
Please write back soon ! *
.... am looking forward to .... letter ! **

Yours, Peter

(*Bitte schreibe bald zurück.
** Ich freue mich auf deinen Brief!)

****

This is Sally .... is new at .... school. .... is tall and thin.
.... eyes are blue and .... hair is long and brown.
.... likes wearing jeans and shirts. .... all like Sally and .... likes .... new friends.

Look, there`s Bob. .... is very strong and clever. .... likes English and German. .... eyes are brown and .... hair is black.
.... isn`t new at .... school. .... like Bob.
What .... says is always funny.

Look, there are Ben and Bill. .... are new in 1c. .... always wear jeans. .... are nice and .... think .... are very cool
.... like Ben and Bill. .... are good friends.
.... bikes are green and blue.

PERSONAL PRONOUNS and POSSESSIVE ADJECTIVES

1. How much is the T-shirt ? ...... is nine pounds.
2. Hi, ... am Jenny ! What`s .... name ?
3. Are ...... okay ? Yes, thanks, ... are fine.
4. Are ....okay ? Yes, thanks, ... am fine.
5. Do .... want a lolly ? No, thank ...., ... hate sweets !
6. Shut ...... book, please.
7. Sorry, ... don`t understand.
8. Here is a photo of .... school. .... all wear uniforms.
9. .... don`t like uniforms. .... think .... look boring.
10. Bend .... knees and shake .... hair !
11. Bill and I are in .... class. .... have got English now.
12. The girls are not at school. .... are at home. .... are ill.
13. Tim likes oranges. .... likes oranges very much.
14. Is this Ben`s satchel ? Yes, ... is .... satchel.
15. The children are at home. .... play hide and seek.
16. Mary is in bed. .... is ill. .... has a cold.
17. Where are Peter and Frank ? .... are not here. I think .... are late.
18. Mother is in the kitchen. .... is baking a cake.
19. Is this .... hanky, Bill ? - No, ... is not .... hanky !
20. Simon and I are good friends. .... are in one class.
21. Mum, are .... books in the kitchen ? - No, ... am sorry !
22. What colour is .... pen, Sarah ? - .... is green.
23. Sue, wipe the ketchup off .... mouth.
24. Are .... alright ? - Yes, ... am OK.
25. Are .... sleepy, Bill ? - No, ... am not.
26. Ben and Frank are late. .... are always late on Mondays.
27. Ann takes a bite of .... hamburger. .... likes hamburgers.
28. .... am Austrian. .... teacher is Mrs Berger.
29. Is .... name Alan ? - No, ... is not. .... is Paul.
30. What colour are .... socks ? .... are red.
31. Our books are green. .... are new.
32. The children have a party. .... like parties.
33. Susan has got many T-shirts. .... likes T-shirts very much.
34. Billy has got a red nose. .... has a cold.
35. Are Sue and Chris at home ? - No, ... are at Sally`s party.
36. What colour is .... schoolbag, Mandy ? - .... is blue.

PERSONAL PRONOUNS and POSSESSIVE ADJECTIVES

1. Billy and Sue have got blue pens. .... are .... pens.
2. Is this a dead mouse ? - No, ... isn`t.
3. Are .... Italian ? - Yes, ... am.
4. Look at the girl over there. .... name is Susan. .... is very nice.
5. .... think .... have a cold.
6. Excuse me, is this .... umbrella ? - No, ... umbrella is green.
7. There is a schoolbag. Is .... schoolbag, Tim ?
8. I have got two pencils. .... are pink and dark green.
9. My brother has got a new bike. .... is blue. .... likes ....
10. The children leave .... shoes in front of the house.
11. This is Sandy`s pen. .... pen is new.
12. Children, eat .... breakfast !
13. The children eat .... breakfast.
14. Sally`s teacher is Mrs Schwarz. .... likes .... teacher.
15. Fill mother`s cup. .... cup is empty.
16. This is .... brother. .... name is Peter. .... is very cool.
17. Sue`s and Bob`s dog is clever. .... dog can open the door.
18. Sally wants an ice cream. .... wants strawberry and vanilla.
19. .... new English book is funny. .... has got many songs.
20. Mick, wipe the chocolate off .... mouth. .... is brown.
21. You and Bill are partners. .... work together.
22. Ben and Bob are partners. .... work together.
23. I and Fred are partners. .... work together.
24. What colour are .... tights ? .... are black.
25. I have got a red cap. .... is .... cap.
26. Where is my rubber ? .... can`t find .... !
27. Pat likes lollies. .... are sweet.
28. Where is the sharpener ? - .... is in .... schoolbag, Peter.
29. Bill, are .... in .... room ? - No, ... am in the kitchen.
30. What colour are .... jeans ? - .... are black.
31. Daniel likes ice cream. .... is sweet.
32. Is Donald hungry ? - Yes .... is.
33. Are .... hungry, Dan ? - No, thanks, ... am not.
34. Tom takes .... coat. .... is cold outside.
35. This is .... house. .... garden is small.
36. Don`t drink father`s wine. .... is .... wine !
37. Is your name Ralph ? - No, ... isn`t. .... is Sandy.

PERSONAL PRONOUNS and POSSESSIVE ADJECTIVES

1. Sarah is ill. .... is in .... room. .... has a bad cold.
2. Conny and .... are good friends. .... are in 1c. .... Maths teacher is nice.
3. The cat and the dog want .... food. .... are hungry.
4. Bob is tired. .... is in .... room.
5. Julia and .... are happy. .... are on .... way to Peter`s party.
6. Sue has a party. .... is .... first party. .... is in the garden with all .... friends.
7. Paul and .... are good friends. .... are in 1c. .... like .... German teacher.
8. The monkeys want .... bananas. .... are very hungry.
9. Tony, can .... touch .... toes ?
10. Tim and .... like exercises. .... can touch .... toes. .... can jump.
11. Tom takes .... umbrella.
12. The green hat is not .... hat ! .... have got a blue hat !
13. The children are in the garden. .... are playing catch.
14. Is this a photo of .... little brother ? - Yes, this is .... baby-brother.
15. Bob and Bill have .... breakfast at eight.
16. What colour is .... schoolbag ? - .... is green.
17. Jack and .... are good friends. .... are in one class. .... play a lot.
18. What is .... name ? - Wuffi !
19. .... English teacher is Mrs Smith. .... is very friendly and nice.
20. Danny, are .... ready ? No, ... am not ! .... can`t find .... shoes !
21. Michael has got a white mouse. .... likes .... mouse very much.
22. Is this .... schoolbag, Bill ? - No .... is not .... schoolbag. .... bag is pink.
23. Where are Phil and Rick ? .... are not here. .... think .... are ill.
24. Liz is four. .... cannot spell .... name.
25. .... are sorry. .... are late.
26. Is .... name Frank ? - No, ... isn`t. .... name is Peter.
27. The children play basketball. .... like ....
28. There is .... sister. .... name is Mary and .... is very nice.
29. .... have got a cat. .... is white and .... nose is pink.
30. .... can`t find .... cat Susan. .... is black and white and .... paws are white, too.

PERSONAL PRONOUNS and POSSESSIVE ADJECTIVES

1. Tom can`t find .... dog Bello. .... is a good dog. .... likes to play. .... ears are white.
2. Where is .... cat ? .... is in the garden and plays with .... ball.
3. .... `ve got two biros. .... are green and blue.
4. Hi, Pam ! How are .... ? - .... am fine, thanks.
5. Look at the snake ! .... mouth is big and .... colour is black and yellow. .... looks ugly.
6. Collin is crazy ! .... hair is green and orange !
7. "Don`t touch .... cigarettes !", father always says.
8. Can .... help .... ? -Yes thanks, ... am new here. .... don`t find the way to .... school.
9. .... have got new jeans. .... are super !
10. Do .... like spearmint gum? - No, ... hate ....
11. Is this .... coat ? - Yes, ... is .... coat.
12. .... mother`s hair is brown. .... like .... hair very much.
13. Can Sally shake .... hair ? - Yes, ... can.
14. Look at .... car ! .... colour is elegant.
15. I can`t eat .... sandwich. Do .... like .... ?
16. John is ill. .... has got stomachache and .... head feels hot.
17. Sandra has got a new dress. .... looks very nice in ....
18. .... new German teacher is Mr Miller. .... is very young.
19. Look at the crocodile ! .... mouth is full of sharp teeth.
20. Don`t take the toffees ! .... are for Mrs. Grant !
21. The children have .... lunch at twelve. .... are very hungry.
22. Paul, are .... ready? - No, Mum, ... can`t find .... schoolbag !
23. Sue is mad ! .... hair is blue and pink.
24. Can .... help me ? - Yes, ... can.
25. Mr Smith`s car is new. .... car is very big. .... is black.
26. ' .... car is very old ', Sam and Eric say.
27. Where is father`s key ? .... key is not there !
28. Tom takes .... umbrella.
29. Sandy likes ...... brother.
30. Is this ...... book, Tim ? Yes it`s ...... book ! Thanks !
31. The green ball is not .... ball. I have a red ball.
32. Excuse me, is this .... hat ? No, it isn`t ......hat ! .... hat is brown !
33. "......... school uniform is nice", Billy says to Tom and Peter.

POSSESSIVE ADJECTIVES

Fill in : *my, your, his, her, its, our, their* :

Simon says:
Bend .... knees ! Raise ....arm ! Stamp ....feet ! Clap .... hands!
Put .... left foot on the chair ! Shake .... hair ! Shake .... head !

Look at Tom ! He shakes .... head. He bends ....knees. He stamps .... feet. He raises .... arms. He puts .... right foot on the table.

Look at Sandra ! She bends ...... knees. She raises ...... left arm. She shakes .... leg. She touches .... nose, ... ears, ...mouth and .... hair.

Look at Bill and Betty ! They touch .... noses, ...eyes, ... knees. They shake .... heads, ... hair,...........arms. They stamp .... feet.

Use possessive adjectives instead of the underlined words:

1. Look at mother\`s dress. .... dress is new.
2. This is my and Peter\`s cat. .... cat is nice.
3. Tim\`s teacher is Mr Smith. He likes .... teacher.
4. This is Mr.Ford\`s car. .... car is red.
5. Listen to Frank\`s and Tina\`s story. .... story isn\`t boring.
6. Cathy\`s party is super ! ...... party is great !!
7. Mother\`s cake is lovely. We love .... cakes !
8. Bring me father\`s pen, please. .... pen is green.
9. This is Billy \`s schoolbag. .... bag is new.
10. Where are the children\`s bikes ? Where are .... bikes ?

HAVE (got) or HAS (got)

I	have	(got) a ball.
You	have	(got) a new car.
He	***has***	(got) a nice sister.
She	***has***	(got) a doll.
It	***has***	(got) a bone.
We	have	(got) a big house.
You	have	(got) a new bike.
They	have	(got) many books.

Have or Has

1. I .... got a blue bag.
2. .... you got a blue bag, too ?
3. You and Tim .... got two red pencils.
4. She .... a long homework today.
5. We ....got English now.
6. I .... got a lot of books at home.
7. Sally .... got fourteen T-shirts.
8. Fred .... a terrible headache.
9. The Millers .... got two children.
10. What .... you got in your pocket ?
11. She .... blue eyes.
12. Frank .... got brown eyes.
13. Our house .... a big garden.
14. Peter .... got three brothers.
15. They .... lots of fun.
16. .... you got a camera ?
17. Sally .... black hair.
18. I .... many toys.
19. The dog .... a big bone.
20. Sarah .... many friends.
21. Ouch ! I .... got toothache !
22. .... you got a pet ? - Yes, I ....
23. We .... enough time.
24. The cat .... a cup of milk for breakfast.
25. How much money .... you got ?
26. I .... got a nice present for you.
27. She .... no time.
28. Peter .... many friends.
29. Father .... not got his key.
30. They .... a nice German teacher.
31. We .... four children.
32. I .... something in my eye.
33. The Smiths .... got a big, black dog.
34. She .... bread and butter for breakfast.
35. Julia .... got a very lovely parrot.

THE VERB

I, we , you, they	**do, go, run, have, eat, sleep, catch, miss, play, try**
He, she, it	**does, goes, runs, has, eats, sleeps, catches, misses, plays, tries**
***Attention*:** **I, you, he, she, it, we, they**	**can, may, must, will, could**

Rule: Don`t forget the third person -s with *he, she, it* !!

1)	run	he runs		
	love	she loves		
	think	he thinks		
	listen	he listens	**- s**	
	read	she reads		
	eat	it eats		
2)	do	he does	**- es**	
	go	she goes		
	catch	it catches		
	miss	he misses		
	watch	she watches	**- es**	nach Zischlauten
	kiss	she kisses		(- s, - sh, - ch)
	pass	it passes		
	finish	he finishes		
	touch	she touches		
	wash	he washes		
3)	buy	he buys		
	say	she says	**- s**	"**y**" nach Vokalen
	stay	he stays		(a,e,i,o,u)
	pay	he pays		wird nicht verwandelt
4)	try	she tries		
	fly	he flies	**- es**	"**y**" nach Konsonanten wird in "**i**" verwandelt

FILL IN THE CORRECT FORM OF THE VERB

1. The mouse .... (hide) in the cupboard.
2. .... (be) you sleepy ? - No, I .... not.
3. How much .... (be) the trousers ? - They .... thirty pounds.
4. Tom .... (take) his brother to school.
5. Lisa and Sam often .... (sit) on the floor and ....(play).
6. Pam .... (wash) her hands and .... (go) to school.
7. We .... (have) got Maths now.
8. Excuse me, where .... (be) Mr Grant ?
9. Sam often .... (miss) the bus.
10. Let`s .... (have) a party. A party .... (be) great fun.
11. Sally .... (wipe) the ketchup off her face.
12. We .... (meet) our friends in the playground.
13. She .... (can) sing a nice song.
14. Tom .... (give) me an apple.
15. I .... (like) ice cream, but Sandy .... (like) fruit.
16. Bob .... (say) hello to his friends.
17. The children .... (sing) a Christmas carol.
18. We .... (buy) schoolthings.
19. Peter .... (come) to my party.
20. The animals .... (be) hungry.
21. The circus director .... (must) feed the animals.
22. We .... (say) hello to our teacher.
23. Sally .... (try) her new blouse on.
24. We .... (try) our new trousers on.
25. We all .... (listen) to the song.
26. The snake .... (be) in front of the door.
27. The baby .... (need) a new jacket.
28. Simon .... (make) a parcel for Ann.
29. We .... (thank) mother for the lovely cake.
30. The children .... (take) out their books and ....(open) them.
31. Ann and Frank .... (go) to a snackbar and .... (buy) a hamburger.
32. Frank .... (pay) for the hamburgers.
33. The children .... (listen) to music.
34. Tim .... (have) a red nose. He .... (have) a bad cold.
35. I ....(can) touch my toes. Paul .... (can) touch his knees.

FILL IN THE CORRECT FORM OF THE VERB

1. What colour .... (be) your socks ?
2. Jill .... (take) her umbrella.
3. Mum and I .... (go) shopping.
4. I .... (want) another coat.
5. Sally .... (order) a big hamburger.
6. He .... (colour) his picture.
7. It .... (look) nice.
8. We .... (meet) Sam and Pam in town.
9. Peter .... (have) a red cap. It .... (go) well with his coat.
10. You .... (can) open the window.
11. The children .... (must) learn the words.
12. Bob .... (jump) and .... (turn) around.
13. Pam .... (wear) a school uniform. She .... (like) it.
14. Jill .... (have) muesli for breakfast.
15. Mary .... (point) at the board.
16. Sandy .... (can) do his homework.
17. The dog .... (hide) its bone under a tree.
18. The cat .... (drink) its milk.
19. Paul .... (want) another slice of cake.
20. Lisa .... (must) go home now. It .... (be) late.
21. Frank .... (have) toothache.
22. The children .... (say), ‘We .... (be) hungry.’
23. The baby .... (cry). It .... (be) sad.
24. Barbara .... (wear) her new trousers to school.
25. Mary .... (go) to the bus at seven, we .... (go) at eight.
26. Your grey trousers .... (look) boring.
27. The pink jacket .... (look) nice.
28. Robert .... (want) another cup of tea.
29. We .... (go) to school at half past seven.
30. Sarah .... (have) got more than a hundred books.
31. I .... (need) a hanky.
32. Oliver often .... (forget) his homework.
33. Mum always .... (ask) the prices when she .... (go) shopping.
34. Mandy .... (love) her orange blouse.
35. We .... (think) our classroom .... (look) nice.
36. Father .... (want) to buy black shoes. He .... (need) new ones.
37. Eric .... (clean) the board.
38. Mary .... (write) a letter.
39. We .... (play) in the living room.

FILL IN THE CORRECT FORM OF THE VERB

1. Mother .... (give) Pat a red apple. He .... (like) apples.
2. She .... (think) orange trousers .... (be) ugly.
3. What colour .... (be) your trousers ?
4. Mary .... (shut) her book and .... (go) to bed.
5. Paul ....(listen) to granny`s story.
6. He .... (hate) sweets. He never .... (have) toothache.
7. We .... (have) got a pot plant in our classroom.
8. Snakes .... (eat) mice and rats.
9. Father .... (go) to the bar with Uncle Bill.
10. Pam .... (have) got a funny little brother.
11. My favourite colours .... (be) blue and green.
12. The monkey .... (dance) in the circus.
13. Ralph .... (hate) lemon juice.
14. The teacher .... (hand) out the homework.
15. Peter always .... (know) the answer.
16. We .... (can) write lots of English words.
17. Jimmy .... (like) toffees, but he .... (hate) chewing gum.
18. Tony .... (run) to school. It .... (be) late.
19. The children .... (have) a party.
20. All friends .... (come) to the party.
21. They .... (eat) hot dogs and cake and .... (drink) orange juice.
22. Peter .... (play) the piano.
23. Father .... (pay) for the lunch in the restaurant.
24. I .... (be) sorry, I .... (must) go home now. It .... (be) six.
25. Peter .... (have) got ninety pence. He .... (want) to buy flowers.
26. Mother .... (make) a parcel for Pit and .... (bake) a cake for him.
27. The clown .... (have) got a funny face.
28. Peter .... (do) his homework in the afternoon.
29. Nora .... (write) a letter to her penfriend.
30. Mother and father .... (make) a trip.
31. Ann .... (try) her new shoes on. They .... (be) dark blue.

Questions

Question with *__is :__*

What **is** your telephone number ? = What`**s** your telephone number ?
What colour **is** your bike ?
Is your phone number correct ?
What **is** your name ? = What`**s** your name ?
What flavour **is** it ?
Is she nice ? Yes, she is. / No she is not. = No, she isn`t.

Question with *__are :__*

Are you hungry ? Yes, I am. / No, I am not.
Are you thirsty ? Yes, I am. / No, I am not.
Are you ready ? Yes, I am. / No, I am not.

Question with *__have got ,has got:__*

Have you **got** a brother ?	Yes, I have. / No, I have not. = No, I haven`t.
Have you **got** a sister ?	Yes, I have. / No, I have not. = No, I haven`t.
Has he **got** a pet ?	Yes, he has. / No, he has not. = No, he hasn`t.

Question with *__do, does :__*

Do you like bananas ?	Yes, I do.	/ No, I do not.	= No, I don`t.
Do you want a lolly ?	Yes, please.	/ No, thank you.	= No, thanks.
Do you go to school ?	Yes, I do.	/ No, I do not.	= No, I don`t.
Does he want a lolly ?	Yes, he does.	/ No, he does not.	= No, he doesn`t.

Questions

Question with <u>can, may, must,will,could</u>:

Can you help me ?	Yes, I can. / No, I ca**nn**ot.	= No, I can`t.
Must we go now ?	Yes, we must.	
May I go to the bus ?	Yes, you may.	
Will you come ?	Yes, I will. / No, I will not.	= No, I won`t.
Could you come at three ?	Yes, I could. / No, I could not.	= No, I couldn`t.

ASKING QUESTIONS

1. He can come.
2. The party is great fun.
3. Sally is happy.
4. The children meet Nora.
5. Sandy must do her homework.
6. The caterpillar is in the grass.
7. The mouse is under the locker.
8. Peter has got a rabbit.
9. The children are in the circus.
10. The monkey is on the elephant.
11. The pullover suits her.
12. Sandra wipes the chocolate off her mouth.
13. All children come to the party.
14. Mick opens the door.
15. Father likes classical music.
16. We all wear uniforms to school.
17. You like grey.
18. Peter goes to school by bus.
19. We go to the Chinese restaurant.
20. Mary buys flowers for Mother`s birthday.
21. Max orders a big hamburger.
22. Sally jumps for joy.
23. The baby puts its toes into its mouth.
24. We are penfriends.
25. My new trousers are red.
26. She wipes the ice cream off her jacket.
27. Peter holds Mary`s hand.
28. She can come in.
29. Fred has got a snake at home.
30. The window is open.
31. The blouse is expensive.
32. Uniforms are boring.
33. Frank is a very nice boy.
34. We must leave now.
35. Her shoes are fifty pounds.
36. Her garden is full of flowers.
37. Willie has got a photo of his cat.
38. Mother likes butterflies.
39. Molly stands up.

ASKING QUESTIONS

1. Fred hates lollies.
2. Billy turns around.
3. Mick Jagger writes a new song.
4. He puts his hand on the table.
5. Mother irons my dress.
6. The teacher hands out our works.
7. Ann meets Mary in front of the house.
8. The pizzaman takes the pizza to the Millers.
9. We often buy ice cream.
10. Her skirt is expensive.
11. We must be quiet in class.
12. Peter must help in the kitchen.
13. You are clever.
14. The parrot eats apples.
15. The monkey eats bananas.
16. The monkeys eat bananas.
17. The pen is in the cupboard.
18. My new coat is in the locker.
19. Peter has got a new bike.
20. Sally must help in the garden.
21. The children play hide and seek.
22. We can spell difficult words.
23. Elephants eat grass.
24. All children like ice cream.
25. Sally has got a nice friend.
26. Paul hates spiders.
27. They are Austrian.
28. Monkeys can climb trees.
29. Phil`s book is boring.
30. We have got many trees in the garden.
31. Mother takes Susan to the piano lesson.
32. The childen often watch TV.
33. Pit listens to the radio.
34. Mary plays with her friend.
35. Father takes Ben to the busstop.
36. Laura likes popcorn.
37. The Millers go to Italy.
38. Nancy can play the recorder.

MIXED EXERCISES

I) Have or has

1. I .... a cat. It .... green eyes.
2. Let`s .... a party.
3. We .... much fun !
4. I .... tea for breakfast.
5. Peter .... a nice T-shirt.
6. They .... red pullovers, Sally .... a green pullover.
7. You ...... got a lovely sister !
8. We .... many friends.

II) Fill in the correct form of the verb:

1. I .... (not, like) her sweater. It .... (be) ugly.
2. .... Jim sad ? No, he .... (not, be).
3. The dress .... (suit) you. I .... (like) it.
4. They .... (take out) a hamburger. They .... (be) hungry.
5. Ann .... (go) to a party.
6. Bob .... (touch) the floor.
7. Tom .... (take) his umbrella.
8. "Shut the books", the teacher .... (say).
9. Sarah .... (jump) and .... (turn) around.
10. The children .... (listen) to music.
11. Peter .... (do) his homework.
12. They .... (be) happy, but Bob .... (be) sleepy.
13. I .... (not, be) sleepy, I .... (be) sad.

III) a / an

1. Tim! Take .... umbrella with you !
2. I have got .... orange pullover, Bill has got .... brown sweater.
3. Have you got .... aunt in America ?
4. My father is .... teacher.
5. There is ...... man in front of the door.

IV) Ask questions:

1. Peter goes to the party.
2. We meet our friends.
3. The teacher hands out the sheets.
4. The monkey takes the banana.
5. Tom is hungry.
6. Tony has got a brother.
7. They are at Sarah`s party.
8. You like bananas.
9. He goes to school.
10. She wants a lolly.
11. We are ready.
12. Tony likes sweets.
13. The cat is on the chair.
14. Pam wants another dress.
15. Mother irons my shirt.
16. They listen to the teacher.
17. I like uniforms.
18. We run to school.

V) They`re , there, their:

1. .... is a letter for you, mum.
2. This is Sam's and Sue' book. It's .... book.
3. .... schoolboys. .... clever.
4. .... schoolbags are heavy.
5. .... is a man at the door.
6. What nationality are they ? .... Austrian.
7. .... are black shoes in front of the door.
8. .... isn't a policeman over there.
9. .... nice girls.
10 .... is a box on the table.
11 What colour are .... shoes ? .... brown.
12 .... is a shoe on the locker !
13 Tom and Pat cannot find .... keys. .... not in the cupboard.
14 .... is a snackbar in front of the park.
15. Oh, ... are .... keys !
16. Tim and his brother are over .... our neighbours.

ITS or IT'S
sein it is

1. .... tail is long.
2. .... a clever cat.
3. .... a new book.
4. .... my pen.
5. What is .... name ? - Rex.
6. .... time for school.
7. .... name is Murli.
8. .... very late.
9. .... Tom' s book.
10. .... nine o'clock.
11. Don't eat the bone! .... bone !
12. The cat has a ball. .... ball.
13. .... a French dog. .... tail is short.
14. .... Bill's class.
15. I have a cat. .... colour is black.
16. .... a red apple.
17. .... a nice dog.
18. .... a clever animal.
19. .... a new grey hat.
20. .... my book. .... new.
21. She has a cat. .... grey.
22. Is it your pen ? - No, ... Bob's
23. .... colour is green.
24. .... name is Blacky.
25. .... Peter's chocolate.
26. .... a tall dog.
27. .... Jane's satchel.
28. We have a hamster. .... six weeks old.
29. Is it .... bone ? - No, ... not .... bone.
30. Ugh ! .... a spider !
31. Is .... name Pongo ? - No, ... Perdita.
32. You have a new shirt. .... nice.
33. .... late, we must go.
34. .... an empty cup.
35. The monkey takes .... banana.
36. .... time for bed, Peter !
37. .... their new song.
38. The dog hides .... bone.

WHAT DO YOU SAY WHEN ....

1. **<u>Du möchtest wissen</u>** wie jemand heißt.
2. . .... wie seine Telephonnummer lautet.
3. . ..... welche Farbe seine Schultasche hat.
4. . .... ob er einen Kaugummi möchte.
5. .... welche Geschmacksrichtung sein Eis hat.
6. ...... ob er fertig ist.
7. ...... ob er Cornflakes mag.
8. ...... welche Farbe seine Hose hat.
9. ...... ob er Joghurt mag.
10....... wieviel das Hemd kostet.
11....... welchen Geschmack der Schlecker hat.
12....... ob er durstig ist.
13...... ob er hungrig ist.
14...... ob er verkühlt ist.
15...... ob er zu deiner Party kommt.
16....... ob du seinen Radiergummi haben kannst.
17....... ob er Orangen mag.
18....... ob er eine Schwester hat.
19........ob er Zahnweh hat.
20 ....ob er müde ist.
21 ....wieviel die Strumpfhose kostet.
22 ....wo deine Feder ist.
23.........was 'Papierkorb' auf Englisch heißt.
24........ wieviel die Kappe kostet.
25.........was Affen essen.
26.........wann er zurückkommt.
27.........wann er seine Hausübung macht.
28........ wo deine neue Bluse ist.
29........ wie es ihm heute geht.
30........ wie sein neuer Englischlehrer heißt.
31........ wie spät es ist.
32........ was es zum Frühstück gibt.
33........ ob er Magenweh hat.
34........ ob er Kopfweh hat.
35........ ob sein Knie schmerzt.
36........ ob er seine Zehen berühren kann.
37........ ob der Papierkorb voll ist.
38........ ob er dir helfen kann.
39........ ob du einen Brieffreund hast.

COMMAND

1)	Let us play ! (Let's play !)	Spielen wir ! (Lasst uns spielen !)
	Let's sing !	Singen wir !
	Let's have a party !	Machen wir eine Party !
	Let's do our homework !	Machen wir unsere Hausübung !
	Let's play hide and seek !	Spielen wir Verstecken !
2)	Shut your books !	Schließt eure Bücher !
	Open the window !	Öffne(t) das Fenster !
	Speak up !	Sprich (Sprecht) lauter !
	Stand up !	Steh(t) auf !
	Be quiet, please !	Sei(d) bitte ruhig !
	Run !	Lauf(t) !
	Go !	Geh(t) !
	Let me see !	Lass(t) mich sehen !
	Let me go now !	Lass(t) mich jetzt gehen !
	Let me help you !	Lass mich dir helfen !
	Leave me alone !	Lass(t) mich in Ruhe !
3)	Don't be so lazy !	Sei(d) nicht so faul !
	Don't go !	Geh(t) nicht !
	Don't be so silly !	Sei(d) nicht so dumm !
	Don't run !	Lauf(t) nicht !
	Don`t keep me waiting !	Lass(t) mich nicht warten !

TRANSLATE

1. Seine Hose ist toll.
2. Ihre Strumpfhose ist alt.
3. Ihre Hose ist gelb.
4. Seine Jeans sind alt.
5. Marys kurze Hose ist rosa.
6. Male einen Schmetterling auf deine Hose !
7. Bügle deine Hose !
8. Ziehe deine Hose an !
9. Die Hose kostet 80 Pfund.
10. Wieviel kostet die Hose ? Sie kostet 90 Pfund.
11. Möchten Sie den Mantel mittelgroß oder groß ?
12. Ich werde ihn ganz groß nehmen.
13. Wieviel kosten die Turnschuhe ? Sie kosten 55 Pfund.
14. Wieviel kostet das T-Shirt mit der Blume darauf ?
15. Es kostet nur 20 Pfund. Das ist billig ! Ich nehme es !
16. Mache einen Kuchen !
17. Mache deine Hausübung!
18. Ihre Hose ist super !
19. Seine kurze Hose ist neu.
20. Meine Strumpfhose ist ok.
21. Ich kann nicht (darf nicht) zu deiner Party kommen.
22. Spielen wir Fangen !
23. Ich habe schrecklich Ohrenweh.
24. Ich habe Husten und Kopfweh.
25. Es geht mir heute nicht sehr gut.
26. Wie geht es dir heute ?
27. Wie fühlst du dich heute ?
28. Kauf den Hund nicht. Er ist zu groß.
29. Lass mich heimgehen !
30. Lass mich sehen !
31. Lass mich in Ruhe !
32. Lass mich nicht warten !
33. Schwätze nicht mit deinem Nachbarn !
34. Gehen wir jetzt !
35. Hilf ihr !
36. Ich habe Halsweh.
37. Spielen wir 'Fang den Dieb'!
38. Es ist fünf nach fünf.
39. Es ist dreiviertel acht.

NEGATION

I am hungry	**I'm not (I am not)** hungry.
You are sad.	**You aren't (You are not)** sad.
He is funny.	**He isn't (He is not)** funny.
Bob **can** come.	Bob **cannot (can't)** come.
He **could** help me.	He **could not (couldn't)** help me.
Pit **eats** ice cream.	Pit **doesn't eat** ice cream.
We **go** to the party.	We **don't go** to the party.
We **do** our homework.	We **don't do** our homework.
He **does** his work.	He **doesn't do** his work.
I **have got** a cat.	I **haven't got (I have not got)** a cat.
He **has got** a dog.	He **hasn't got (Has not got)** a dog.
I **have** a good mark.	I **don't have (I haven't got)** a good mark.
She **has** a nice brother.	She **doesn't have (hasn't got)** a nice brother.

NEGATION

1. I have got a brother.
2. He is a nice boy.
3. We go to a party.
4. She writes a letter.
5. We are happy.
6. They are sad.
7. He sings a song.
8. He has got a pencil.
9. I go to his party.
10. Cathy is hungry.
11. Peter is in the garden.
12. We say "Hello".
13. You run to Peter.
14. She goes to town.
15. We are hungry.
16. She has got a sister.
17. We have got a new pullover.
18. They eat a cake.
19. Ann bends her knees.
20. Mother irons my shirt.
21. They listen to the teacher.
22. Pam wants new trousers.
23. They listen to the music.
24. Tony likes ice cream.
25. The monkey takes the banana to the baby monkey.
26. We eat a cake.
27. They touch the floor.
28. It is nice.
29. This is a photo of our school.
30. I like uniforms.
31. Bob is clever.
32. I have got a pet.
33. His hair is black.
34. Tom has got a pet.
35. We iron our shirts.
36. My sister irons my blouse.
37. Children love sweets.

38. Sandy stands up.
39. Billy jumps high.
40. The cat is on the chair.
41. You are in the garden.
42. We are at home.
43. We eat a sandwich.
44. She wants a lolly.
45. My brother goes to school.
46. You like bananas.
47. Come to Bob !
48. Let`s go to the circus !
49. Peter goes to the party.
50. You run fast.
51. Sally writes a poem.
52. Tony has got a brother.
53. We meet our friends.
54. The cat is hungry.
55. We are sleepy.
56. He likes jeans.
57. He is a funny teacher.
58. Sarah is nice.
59. We wear uniforms.
60. I like wearing skirts.
61. He is new at our school.
62. I think he is nice.
63. He looks at the photo.
64. He is cool.
65. His eyes are blue.
66. His name is Smith.
67. I like our school.
68. She likes wearing trousers.
69. We turn around.
70. She opens the window.
71. Tim is quiet.
72. Liz shuts the book.
73. The frog is behind the curtain.
74. He takes the book to Peter.
75. I love toffees.
76. The monkey eats popcorn.
77. They catch the thief.

78. Elephants eat grass.
79. Snakes love eggs.
80. He stamps his feet.
81. I`ve got toothache.
82. My knee hurts.
83. Be quiet !
84. Let`s write a song !
85. Shut the window !
86. Stand up !
87. Turn around !
88. Shake your hair !
89. Let`s play hide and seek !
90. Go to the blackboard !
91. Peter likes hamburgers.
92. Ann is at home.
93. He likes wearing dark colours.
94. Sit down !
95. Mandy has got a sister.
96. She is lovely.
97. We go to a restaurant.
98. He runs to school.
99. She likes apples very much.
100. I like coffee.
101. Pam opens the door.
102. Pit is ill.
103. Father works in the garden.
104. The children play hide and seek.
105. It is a wonderful day.
106. I buy a toothbrush.
107. Frank eats strawberries.
108. Pamela likes popcorn.
109. We go to the circus.
110. The frog jumps into the pond.
111. Mother makes a plan for the week.
112. We write a list.
113. The children go to the playground.
114. The girls play with their dolls.
115. I have got a brother and a sister.
116. He can jump around.
117. Peter can open the box.

PLURAL

1) apple	⇨	apples	
pen	⇨	pens	
desk	⇨	desks	**An das Hauptwort wird "s" angehängt.**
book	⇨	books	

2) bus	⇨	buses	
kiss	⇨	kisses	
fox	⇨	foxes	**Nach einem Zischlaut (-s, -sh, -ch, -x, -z) wird "es" angehängt.**
watch	⇨	watches	
sandwich	⇨	sandwiches	
bush	⇨	bushes	
brush	⇨	brushes	

3) city	⇨	cities	
lady	⇨	ladies	
fly	⇨	flies	**Nach Mitlaut und "y" wird das "y" in "ie" verwandelt.**
lolly	⇨	lollies	
story	⇨	stories	
baby	⇨	babies	

4) boy	⇨	boys	
day	⇨	days	**Nach Selbstlaut und "y " bleibt das "y" erhalten.**
toy	⇨	toys	

5) wife	⇨	wives	
knife	⇨	knives	**"f" wird zu "v"**
shelf	⇨	shelves	**Ausnahmen:**
wolf	⇨	wolves	roof ⇨ roofs
life	⇨	lives	chief ⇨ chiefs
calf	⇨	calves	handkerchief ⇨ handkerchiefs
loaf	⇨	loaves	cliff ⇨ cliffs
leaf	⇨	leaves	
thief	⇨	thieves	

PLURAL

6) man	⇨	**men**	
woman	⇨	**women**	
child	⇨	**children**	
mouse	⇨	**mice**	
foot	⇨	**feet**	**unregelmäßige Bildung**
tooth	⇨	**teeth**	
goose	⇨	**geese**	
louse	⇨	**lice**	
ox	⇨	**oxen**	

7) tomato	⇨	tomato**es**
potato	⇨	potato**es**
piano	⇨	pianos
photo	⇨	photos
Eskimo	⇨	Eskimos

8) trousers
jeans
pants
tights
scissors
glasses

Nur Pluralform

9) fish
sheep
deer

Nur Singularform

FORM THE CORRECT PLURALS

story	....	toe	....
box	....	lolly	....
monkey	....	star	....
dress	....	apple	....
toothbrush	....	woman	....
man	....	book	....
mouse	....	toffee	....
orange	....	desk	....
sandwich	....	fruit gum	....
camera	....	boy	....
strawberry	....	party	....
class	....	box	....
inch	....	child	....
foot	....	tooth	....
goose	....	knife	....
wolf	....	calf	....
crocodile	....	lady	....
city	....	life	....
watch	....	kiss	....
bus	....	fly	....
bush	....	glass	....
fox	....	ox	....
horse	....	fish	....
match	....	key	....
wife	....	toy	....
day	....	tomato	....
potato	....	Eskimo	....
cliff	....	leaf	....
roof	....	thief	....
berry	....	baby	....
louse	....	pen	....
fish	....	sheep	....
deer	....	handkerchief	....
photo	....	satchel	....
house	....	glass	....
cow	....	brush	....
teacher	....	car	....

dog	....	door	....
painter	....	bike	....
computer	....	shelf	....
pencil	....	pupil	....
sharpener	....	note	....
recorder	....	dialogue	....
brother	....	banana	....
cup	....	cap	....
tree	....	dream	....

TRANSLATE:

1) Fische schwimmen im Fluß.
2) Unsere Schafe fressen Gras.
3) Meine Hose ist toll !
4) Seine Zähne schmerzen.
5) Mäuse mögen Käse.
6) Die Füchse fangen die Gänse.
7) Füchse verstecken sich in Büschen.
8) Wölfe sind gefährlich.
9) Alle Blätter fallen vom Baum.
10) Viele Hunde haben Läuse.
11) Die Gläser sind voll.
12) Wo ist Tim`s Hose ?
13) Meine Füße schmerzen.
14) Die Geschichten sind interessant.
15) Die Regale sind lang.
16) Wir fangen die Diebe.
17) Magst du Erdbeeren ?
18) Die Babies weinen.
19) Mäuse sind klein.
20) Verstecken wir uns hinter den Büschen.
21) Meine Brille ist neu.
22) Meine Strumpfhose ist schwarz.
23) Fliegen sind hässlich.
24) Wieviele Sandwiches isst er?
25) Schlecker sind süß.
26) Ich liebe Tomaten.
27) Ich kaufe zwei Brotlaibe.

SHORT FORMS

I am ill.	I**'m** ill.
You are sad.	You**'re** sad.
He is lazy.	He**'s** lazy.
She is nice.	She**'s** nice.
It is lovely.	It**'s** lovely.
What is the time ?	What**'s** the time?
There is a cat.	There**'s** a cat.
We are friendly.	We**'re** friendly.
You are happy.	You**'re** happy.
They are rich.	They**'re** rich.

I have a brother.	I**'ve** a brother.
He has a dog.	He**'s** a dog.

OK. I will take it.	OK. I**'ll** take it.

Let us play.	Let**'s** play.

's = is, has, us

It is not too late.	It **isn't** too late.
They are not at home.	They **aren't** at home.
I have not got a sister.	I **haven't** got a sister.
He has not got a cat.	He **hasn't** got a cat.
I cannot come.	I **can't** come.
I will not take the shirt.	I **won't** take the shirt.

<u>Short answers</u>:

Are you hungry ?	Yes, **I am.** (**NOT**: *I'm.*)	No, **I'm** not.
Is he nice ?	Yes, **he is.** (**NOT**: *he's.*)	No, he **isn't.**
Is there a cat ?	Yes, **there is.** (**NOT**: *There's.*)	No, there **isn't.**
Does he sleep ?	Yes, he **does.**	No, he **doesn't.**
Do you like tea ?	Yes, I **do.**	No, I **don't.**

SHORT ANSWERS

Answer with 'Yes' and 'No':

1. Are you Austrian ?
2. Is he late ?
3. Is Pintu an Indian name ?
4. Are we late ?
5. Are Fred and Sue English ?
6. Can you speak English ?
7. Have you got a pocket calculator ?
8. Can the boys play football ?
9. Has Pam got a computer game ?
10. Are Phil and Ralph twins ?
11. Have Sandy and Rick got a school uniform ?
12. Can I stay with you ?
13. Do you like coffee ?
14. Is her uniform nice ?
15. Have you got a pet ?
16. Can you help me ?
17. Is there a bird in the tree ?
18. Is the postman at the gate ?
19. Do you want to play ?
20. Are you tired ?
21. Is there milk in the fridge ?
22. Can Bob find his keys ?
23. Have you got a new dress ?
24. Can you jump off the chair ?
25. Do you often listen to the radio ?
26. Does he often watch TV ?
27. Has Peter got a bike ?
28. Can you turn on the radio ?
29. Do you like computer games ?
30. Is Ben your brother ?
31. Are you good at skiing ?
32. Is he good at singing ?
33. Do you want an orange ?
34. Does Bill write a letter ?
35. Does he go away ?
36. Can you shout ?

PERSONAL PRONOUNS (OBJECT FORM)

I	**me**
you	**you**
he	**him**
she	**her**
it	**it**
we	**us**
you	**you**
they	**them**

Before the verb :

I, you, he, she, it, we, you, they

After the verb:

me, you, him, her, it, us, you, them

Can **you** help **me** ?
I can see **you**.
We meet **him**.
We see **her**.
I like **it**.
She helps **us**.
You greet **them**.

PERSONAL PRONOUNS (+ Object form) AND POSSESSIVE ADJECTIVES

1. Your feet aren't clean. Go and wash your feet !
2. Read your book.
3. Buy some apples.
4. Take the letter to the post office. Take the parcels, too.
5. We all like comics.
6. Look at the children !
7. Listen to the child !
8. They meet Mrs and Mr Clark.
9. There is a parcel for the boys.
10. He eats a sandwich.
11. She buys two new dresses.
12. They play with Sally and Sue.
13. Do you see the children ?
14. Look at the flowers.
15. She likes her blouses.
16. Father buys a new car.
17. Open your satchel.
18. Sally draws a house.
19. The children have got a record.
20. Mother prepares dinner.
21. Show your homework to Mr Smith.
22. Bob and I listen to records.
23. Look at my nice pictures.
24. Show your tests to your teacher.
25. Help your little brother.
26. Take the apples to the animals.
27. Give the ball to mother.
28. Your hands are dirty. Go and wash your hands !
29. Look at Sue`s hat. The hat is funny !
30. Bring father Paul`s and Bill`s books.
31. You and your brother are hungry.
32. I and my sister are tired.
33. Sandy and Sue meet their teachers.
34. Give Billy and me two apples.
35. Where is Sandy ? Here is .... blouse.
36. Have you got John`s kite ? No, ... kite is in the classroom.
37. Where are Bill and Tom ? There are only .... shoes.

38. There are Peggy and Tony ! Don`t show .... the sweets !
39. I`ve got a lot of Italian stamps. I can give .... to you.
40. The children are eating .... sandwiches.
41. Is Sally at home ? Yes, she`s in .... room.
42. Hi Tom ! Do you want to see .... collection of stones ?
43. Peter ! Show .... new bicycle, please !
44. Is this Joe`s rubber ? Yes, I think .... is .... rubber !
45. Sue is hungry. Give .... an apple, please.
46. Where are the pencils ? .... are in the box.
47. Look at Tim and me ! Look at ...... !
48. We are thirsty. Can you give .... some water ?
49. I want this dress. Can I buy .... ?
50. There is a mouse under the locker. Can you see .... ?
51. Excuse .... , what's the time ?
52. Bob wants a drink. Please, give .... a glass of milk.
53. Father, there is a letter for .... !
54. Nancy and Sue are my best friends. .... like .... very much.
55. Where are the keys ? I can't find ....
56. Where is Mum ? - .... is in the kitchen.
57. The children hide in the garden. I don't see ....
58. Peter, please help .... with my homework.
59. Father, please help .... with our homework. We can't do .... !
60. Tom, there is a present for .... from Uncle Mark !
61. Mother cannot open the tin. Can you help .... ?
62. I' ve got a Matchbox car for Peter and Sue has got sweets for ....
63. Do .... know where my new pencils are ? I don't find .... !
64. I don't like cheeseburgers. I really hate ....
65. Look at Betty ! .... is very sad. Let's ask .... if we can help ....!
66. She is on .... way home.
67. I go to Frank. I must show .... my new game boy !
68. The photo is nice ! Give .... to the Millers.
69. Mum, I need new trousers. I really need ....
70. Do you like fishburgers ? - No I hate ....
71. Bob is on .... way to school.
72. Mum, where are my shoes ? I can't find ....
73. Can you open the bottle ? I can' t do .... !
74. Let's hide Sally's trainers. Let's hide .... in her satchel.
75. Tell me what's in the box ! Oh, please, tell me what's in .... !
76. Do you like spinach ? No, I don't like .... very much.
77. Robert writes a letter to .... penfriend. He often writes to ....

PERSONAL PRONOUNS (+ Object form) AND POSSESSIVE ADJECTIVES

1. Tomorrow is Jane`s birthday. She wants to invite all .... friends.
2. We are hiding behind the door. Peter cannot see ....
3. .... brushes .... teeth every morning.
4. Bill and Michael are playing with .... computer games.
5. It`s mother`s birthday. Let`s buy some flowers for ....
6. Pit, ... wish .... all the best !
7. .... comb their hair.
8. .... combs her hair.
9. We are looking for .... dog.
10. Bill is in bed. Bring .... a cup of tea.
11. Betty, is this .... pen ? Yes, thanks, ... is ! .... have got a red one.
12. Here are Mrs and Mr Brown. .... are Peter`s parents.
13. Betty is looking for .... book. She cannot find ....
14. Bob, there is some cake for ....
15. Where is the Millers` house ? I must bring .... a letter.
16. Look ! The bird is sleeping in .... nest.
17. Susan goes to Bill. She brings .... a book.
18. Look at the crocodile ! Do you see .... teeth ?
19. Bill ! Wash .... hands !
20. It`s .... birthday. Granny wishes me a happy birthday.
21. The children don`t understand. Let`s help ....
22. Hi, Robert ! Can I come to .... today ?
23. When you are in England, please write a letter to ....
24. In the morning we wash .... faces and brush .... teeth.
25. We don`t know how to turn on the tape recorder.
    Can .... help ....?
26. We are looking for Pit and Tom. Can you see ....?
    Or can you see .... bikes ?
27. Sally knows where they are ! Ask .... !
28. Helen is my best friend. I like .... very much !
29. We are hungry. Please, give ...... something to eat.
30. Is this Pat`s coat ? Yes .... is .... coat. .... has got a green coat.
31. I want to see your collection. Please, let ..... see ....
32. Look at Uncle Ben`s car ! ..... is dirty and .... tyres are flat !
33. Peter and Mary cannot find .... tickets. Let`s help ....
34. Where are our tickets ? We can`t find ....

35. Where is Betty ? I`d like to speak to ....
36. The football is not here. We must look for ....
37. Can you see Mr Smith ? I must speak to ....
38. Do .... know where my pants are ? I can`t find ....
39. What have you got for Fred ? .... have got a book for ....
40. I am thirsty. Please, give .... a coke.
41. This is an interesting book. .... like .... very much.
42. He can`t buy this car. .... is too expensive for ....
43. I know that you`re hiding behind the bushes, but ........ can`t see ....
44. Have you got a present for the children ?
    Yes, ... have got a ball for .... I hope, they'll like ....
45. I can`t come to your party, but there is a present for ....
46. The party is at the Coopers` house.
    I think, I `ll buy some flowers for ....
47. This present is for Bob. Can you give .... to .... , please ?
48. Where are the children ? I don't know, but .... must be here,
    .... coats are over there .
49. Maggy has lots of posters of the Kelly Family in .... room.
50. Is Ben at home ? - Yes, ... is up in .... room.
    .... is doing .... homework. Go and help ....
51. Who is that girl over there ? Do you know .... ?
52. Let's hide behind the sofa. Bob won't find .... !
53. Where is the dog ? .... is in the garden.
54. Hi, Frank ! How are .... ? - .... am fine, thank .... !
55. Where is Pam ? .... shoes are there, but .... isn't there.
56. The cigarettes are for father. .... are for ....
57. .... often sing songs in English.
58. Nancy and I are good friends. .... are in one class.
59. Mark has got new trousers. .... thinks .... are very cool.
60. Sue, give .... my book , please ! - Here .... are.
61. How old are ...., Bill ? - .... am seven.
62. Barbara is small. .... cannot write .... name.
63. Uncle Bill smokes a lot. .... smokes 30 cigarettes a day.
64. Mary and I love tennis. .... play three times a week.
65. I like these jeans. How much are .... ?
66. Mr Smith has got an old car. .... is fifteen years old.
67. What's that terrible smell ? .... comes from the kitchen.
68. Mother is baking a cake. .... will be lovely. .... is a good cook.
69. I love the Scorpions. Do .... like .... , too ?
70. Tom's gloves are not there. We must look for ....

PERSONAL PRONOUNS (+ Object form) AND POSSESSIVE ADJECTIVES

1. Look at the shoes !
2. Maggie has three apples.
3. Billy is a new boy in our class.
4. The children have new books.
5. Mrs Williams has an old car.
6. Give that letter to Mother.
7. Your shoes are nice.
8. Take that bag.
9. Bill's father is a policeman.
10. The cat is small.
11. Open your bag, please.
12. Show your homework to the teacher.
13. There is a bill for mother.
14. Put Dad's hat on.
15. Look at Billy.
16. Look at the children.
17. The postman is at the door.
18. Your pencils are on the desk.
19. I and my sister are tired.
20. We meet our teacher.
21. We meet our teachers.
22. Bob and Bill are clever.
23. Give the book to Tim.
24. Her cup is empty.
25. Our books are heavy.
26. Tom and Bill look at Sandy.
27. Bill and I must look for Bob.
28. Please, help me and Ben.
29. This is Mary's satchel.
30. You and Liz eat sandwiches.
31. We like our neighbours very much.
32. Write a letter to Aunt Betty and Uncle Bill.
33. Do you like my and Frank's records ?
34. Peter listens to his new records.
35. Mother loves her children.
36. The children give a red rose to mother.
37. Give the cap to Jeff.

PRESENT TENSE SIMPLE FORM

Wir verwenden die **Simple Form** zum Ausdruck von:

Gewohnheiten	I always go to bed at 8 pm.
Tatsachen	The earth turns around the sun.
Gedanken	I think he is right.
Gefühlen	I like him.
wiederholten Handlungen	He often watches TV in the evening.

Signalwörter:

often
always
never
as a rule
again and again
every day, month, week, year, summer, winter .....
every weekend, Monday, English lesson ......
usually
generally
normally
sometimes
rarely
seldom
whenever
On Mondays, Tuesdays .....

PRESENT TENSE PROGRESSIVE FORM

Wir verwenden diese Form für Handlungen, die **jetzt gerade** geschehen, oder für **Ausnahmehandlungen** :

I **am writing** a letter **now**. (Jetzt gerade)
Ben usually goes to school by bus, **but today he is running.** (Ausnahme)

I	**am working.**
You	**are writing.**
He	**is singing.**
She	**is running.**
It	**is eating** a bone.
We	**are jumping**.
You	**are playing.**
They	**are swimming.**

Signalwörter :

now
at the moment
at present
still
just
Look !
Listen !

1) Stummes "e" entfällt vor -ing Form:

com**e**	coming
writ**e**	writing
danc**e**	dancing
rid**e**	riding

2) Der Mitlaut nach kurzen Vokalen wird verdoppelt:

cu**t**	cu**tt**ing
ho**p**	ho**pp**ing
ru**n**	ru**nn**ing
si**t**	si**tt**ing
swi**m**	swi**mm**ing
hi**t**	hi**tt**ing
dro**p**	dro**pp**ing

3) "y" vor -ing Form bleibt erhalten:

bu**y**	bu**y**ing
fl**y**	fl**y**ing
cr**y**	cr**y**ing
pa**y**	pa**y**ing
pla**y**	pla**y**ing

4) "ie" wird in "y" verwandelt:

l**ie**	l**y**ing
d**ie**	d**y**ing

Die -ing Form wird **normalerweise** ***nicht*** verwendet mit:

want, love, like, hate, dislike, prefer, desire, wish, need, know, understand, remember, forget, recognize, expect, mean, see, hear, smell, taste

SIMPLE FORM OR - ING FORM ?

1. What .... (Tom /do) ? He .... (write) a letter.
2. Sandy .... (be) always late.
3. Look, Peter .... (juggle).
4. Sally never .... (speak) to me.
5. We seldom .... (watch) TV, but now I .... (watch) a film.
6. The shops .... (open) at eight and .... (close) at six pm.
7. Every day he .... (start) to work at eight and he .... (come) home at six pm.
8. She always .... (go) to work by car.
9. Listen, the boy .... (sing) a nice song !
10. They usually .... (have) dinner at seven.
11. I sometimes .... (feel) sad.
12. Ann often .... (play) tennis. She`s really good at playing tennis !
13. Mother rarely .... (go) out in the evening, but today she .... (have) a party.
14. Pst ! The baby .... (sleep) ! Don`t be so loud !
15. The earth .... (move) round the sun.
16. She .... (be) clever. She .... (speak) four languages.
17. Tom always .... (get) up at six. He .... (have) his breakfast at seven and then he .... (go) to work.
18. What .... (you / do) ? I .... (listen) to the radio !
19. He usually .... (go) to work by bus.
20. Jack .... (not / eat) very much. He never .... (have) breakfast in the morning.
21. The weather here .... (not / be) very good. It often .... (rain).
22. Pit .... (smoke) ten cigarettes a day.
23. I rarely .... (go) to bed before midnight.
24. She .... (not / eat) meat very often.
25. Listen ! Pat .... (play) the piano !
26. They .... (have) their lunch at the moment.
27. Look ! Somebody .... (swim) in the cold river !

28. Mum !!! Help me, please ! - I ....(come) !
29. .... (it / snow) now?
No, it .... (rain).
30. You .... (stand) on my foot ! Oh, very sorry !
31. Hurry up ! The bus .... (come) !
32. Call in the evening ! We usually .... (stay) at home in the evenings.
33. Molly never .... (speak) to me.
34. Where .... (you / usually / spend) your holidays ?
We always .... (fly) to Greece.
35. What ....(you / do) ? - I ....(look for) my key !
36. Peter .... (wash) his hair every day.
37. Peter must .... (wash) his hair twice a week.
38. She ....(do) her shopping on Monday, as a rule, but today she .... (stay) at home, because she .... (have) a cold.
39. How often .... (he / drink) coffee a day ? - Never !
40. Jill .... (play) the guitar, but she .... (not / play) now.
41. Please, be quiet ! I .... (work). I .... (must/ work) so much !
42. He usually .... (read) a book in the evening, but this evening he .... (listen) to the radio.
43. We generally .... (have) breakfast in the morning, but today we .... (only drink) a cup of black tea.
44. He rarely .... (play) in the playground, but this afternoon he .... (play) there.
45. Listen ! Bob .... (listen to) records.
46. Every morning Peter .... (clean) his teeth.
47. Look ! That girl over there .... (wait) for her brother.
48. Babies often .... (play) with their toes.
49. Don`t disturb me ! I .... (do) my homework.
50. Don`t talk to him now. He .... (write) a letter to his pen friend.
51. Listen ! Our teacher .... (tell) a funny story.
52. Boys .... (like) to climb steep rocks.
53. Look ! The monkey .... (climb up) a high tree.

SIMPLE FORM OR -ING FORM ?

1. Sarah .... (have) a shower at the moment.
2. Take an umbrella. It .... (rain).
3. You can turn off the radio. I .... (not / listen).
4. Why are you on the locker ? What .... (you / do) ??
5. Bob always .... (drink) tea in the morning.
6. Father usually .... (read) a book in the evening.
7. He generally .... (finish) his homework at three, but today he .... (still write) a long letter.
8. I can see him: he .... (sit) on a chair and he .... (read).
9. Where are the children ? They .... (play) in the garden.
10. We .... (have) dinner now. Can you .... (phone) a bit later ?
11. Hey ! You .... (not / listen) to me !
12. Don`t you hear it ! The telephone .... (ring) !
13. You can turn the TV off. I .... (not / watch).
14. I .... (stay) in bed because I`m ill.
15. Where are you ? - Here in the kitchen ! I ....(have) my meal !
16. On the telephone: Hello, can I .... (speak) to Mary, please ? She .... (have) a shower, can you .... (phone) later ?
17. On Mondays she .... (go) for a walk in the park.
18. Father usually .... (finish) work at six p.m. but today he .... (still / work).
19. Oh no ! It .... (still / rain) ! So we .... (not / can / go) out.
20. I usually .... (go) to bed early, but today I .... (still read) an interesting book.
21. George usually .... (go) to work by bus, but today he .... (walk).
22. Jack .... (drive) to Italy every summer.
23. Listen, a bird .... (sing) in the tree !
24. Mother .... (read) the newspaper every morning, but today she .... (clean) the windows.
25. It .... (be) always cold in winter.

26. Pat always .... (feel) happy.
27. .... (you / often / eat) in restaurants ? - No, not very often.
28. The train .... (arrive) at six, as a rule.
29. Tim usually .... (have) muesli for breakfast, but this morning he .... (eat) his birthday cake.
30. I .... (have) my piano lesson on Mondays.
31. She .... (not / do) her homework at the moment, she .... (phone) her friend.
32. In autumn, the leaves .... (fall) from the trees.
33. Sandy often .... (go) away at the weekend.
34. What ....(you / usually / do) at the weekend ? Oh, not very much: I .... (read) a book or I .... (watch) TV or I .... (play).
35. Paul never.............................. (feel) sad again.
36. He likes this video. He .... (watch) it again and again.
37. I can never .... (find) my keys.
38. She rarely .... (meet) him.
39. Every Friday mother .... (bake) a fine cake.
40. Look ! They .... (sit) in a very fast car.
41. A real gentleman .... (open) the door for a lady.
42. She has no time now. She .... (do) her homework.
43. He .... (do) his homework at two p.m. every afternoon.
44. She always .... (go) shopping on Mondays but today she .... (have) a chat with her neighbour.
45. Look ! The children .... (run) to school.
46. John .... (walk) to school every day. This is healthy, he always .... (say).
47. I .... (do) an exercise now.
48. They .... (have) their tea at the moment.
49. Tim .... (watch) TV every afternoon.
50. The children .... (play) in their room. They can`t .... (come) now.
51. I must .... (do) my homework now.
52. Can you .... (help) me now ? Sorry, I can`t. I .... (feed) the baby !
53. What .... (you / eat) ? I .... (eat) a lovely cake !
54. I must .... (shut) the window now. It`s so cold.

SIMPLE FORM OR -ING FORM ?

1. Can I .... (ask) you something ? Not now, I .... (listen to) the song on the cassette.
2. Don`t talk to her now. She .... (write) a letter to her friend.
3. Bill .... (walk) to school every day. Sally .... (go) by bike.
4. Look, the boys .... (ride) their bikes.
5. Fred, can you .... (help) me with my homework ? I`m sorry, I can`t, I .... (test) the new computer game.
6. What ....(you / eat) ? I .... (eat) an apple.
7. Sandy usually .... (watch TV) in the afternoon.
8. I always .... (get up) at six in the morning and then I .... (have) a big breakfast.
9. Peter .... (go) to school at seven every morning.
10. I always .... (get) home at four.
11. We never .... (watch) TV in the evening.
12. We must .... (go) to bed at eight.
13. I .... (do) my homework after lunch every day.
14. Mother usually .... (go) to bed at eleven, but today she .... (watch) an interesting film on TV.
15. We always .... (wash) our hands before dinner.
16. Grandma never .... (go) to the cinema. She always .... (stay) at home.
17. Our neighbour`s dog always .... (bark) at night.
18. Our cat never .... (catch) mice.
19. Every birthday Mum .... (get) nice flowers.
20. Pam .... (like) ice cream better than pudding.
21. Look at him ! He`s so young and he .... (smoke).
22. Listen ! The Kelly Family .... (sing).
23. At present my father .... (work) in his office.
24. We .... (do) an exercise about present progressive now.
25. Look out of the window ! It .... (snow).
26. Peter .... (collect) minerals and stamps.
27. The boys .... (run) to the park now.

28. Uncle Marc .... (visit) us every year.
29. Look, it .... (start) to rain.
30. He always .... (bring) nice things.
31. You can`t .... (speak) to her now, because she .... (sleep).
32. Listen ! The baby .... (cry). Babies .... (cry) very often.
33. We often .... (look) at the stars at night.
34. Why .... (you / look) at me ? I think, I .... (know) you.
35. I often .... (think) of you.
36. Cats usually .... (eat) mice.
37. I can`t .... (come) with you.
I .... (play).
38. You must .... (drink) your lemonade when it is hot.
39. Sally ! - I can`t .... (come) now !
I .... (look for) my key ! I can`t .... (find) it !
40. He usually .... (go) to bed at nine, but today he .... (stay) up because there`s a good film on TV.
41. .... (you / see) the man over there ?
He .... (wear) a funny hat !
42. Mother rarely .... (go) to town on Friday, she sometimes .... (go) on Wednesday.
43. Can you .... (come) to me now ? - No, I am sorry !
I .... (bake) a cake. So I must .... (stay) at home now.
44. Are you ready ? - Yes, I ....am coming.... (come) !
45. Mary often ....writes.............. (write) letters. At the moment she ....is writting............. (write) a letter to her penpal.
46. Bill and his sister always ......do................. (do) their homework in the afternoon.
47. Be quiet, please. Mum and Dad ....are listening to.... (listen to) the news on the radio.
48. Don’t disturb me ! I am watching................. (watch) a film.
49. Where is the cat ? It ....is running................. (run) after a mouse.
50. Tom and Sue ......go..................... (go) to the bus at seven every morning.
51. He always ....washes................. (wash) his hands before lunch.
52. Can I .....asks.................... (ask) you something ?

HOW TO ASK QUESTIONS

We live **in Austria.**
Where do we live ?

They go to bed **at 8 pm.**
When do they go to bed ?

He washes his hair **once a week.**
How often does he wash his hair ?

The blouse is **three pounds.**
How much is the blouse ?

He eats **three** sandwiches.
How many sandwiches does he eat ?

I usually **play football** at weekends.
What do you usually do at weekends ?

He is doing **his homework** now.
What is he doing now ?

Mary **is playing** in the garden now.
What is Mary doing now ?

Robert goes to school.
Who goes to school ? (Question with **who / what**
1. Fall N O DO !!!!)

We like **Mr Crisp.**
Who <u>do</u> we like ? (4.Fall)

A red rose grows in front of my window every year.
What grows in front of my window every year ? (1.Fall)

A tree is standing behind the house.
What is standing behind the house ?

She is looking for **her shoes**.
What is she looking <u>for</u> ?

He looks at **me**.
Who does he look <u>at</u> ?

Sandy eats **some cake.**
What does Sandy eat ? (4.Fall)

This is **Bill`s** model plane.
Whose model plane is this ?

Their uniforms are **blue.**
What colour are their uniforms ?

Her blouse is **pink.**
What colour is her blouse ?

He always goes to work **by car.**
How does he go to work ?

He likes **chocolate** cake best.
What kind of cake does he like best ?

She prefers **vanilla** icecream.
What flavour does she prefer ?

Their car is **a Ford.**
What make is their car ?

QUESTIONS

1. We often run to school in the morning.
2. Sandy eats my sandwich.
3. Father buys the newspaper every evening.
4. The girl can sing a lot of songs.
5. We are watching TV in the afternoon.
6. Bill is not good at climbing trees.
7. They always have bread and butter for breakfast.
8. Mother always listens to the news at seven o`clock.
9. We have got English five times a week.
10. Sandy has got a new model plane.
11. We are just working in the garden.
12. He likes Bob`s sister.
13. Pat wants to have the blue ball.
14. Maggie is paying for the stamps.
15. You must help me with the homework, because I can`t do it alone.
16. You can have my apple.
17. The children play near the river every day.
18. We must look for Tom.
19. Sandy looks for his keys.
20. He cannot eat everything.
21. Bob likes to jump high.
22. The aeroplane is flying over the town.
23. Tom likes to jump into the water.
24. The children go to a birthday party at Mary`s house.
25. His satchel is blue.
26. The girl helps her mother in the kitchen.
27. The cat is holding a mouse between its teeth.
28. Milly has got a nice little cat.
29. Peter goes to bed , because he is tired.
30. The boy wants some ice cream.
31. Trish loves strawberry cake.
32. We do our homework after school.
33. They listen to good music.
34. She has got new jeans.
35. The dog runs after the ball.
36. We visit our grandma in the holidays.
37. They brush their teeth before they go to bed.
38. There is a letter for Tim.
39. We wait for the bus every morning.

40. I love her little sister.
41. The plane leaves at 6 pm.
42. She is waiting for her friend.
43. He gets a present from his uncle every birthday.
44. Ann listens to Bill`s cassette in bed.
45. Our school uniform is blue.
46. The trousers are 30 pounds.
47. Mother sews a new dress for Mary.
48. I always go to town on Saturday.
49. Peter likes Ann`s books.
50. The children buy food every Friday.
51. Tom can sing many songs.
52. Tony is listening to the cassette.
53. Bob is good at skiing.
54. We always have muesli for breakfast.
55. Father always listens to the news at eight o`clock.
56. We are always at school in the morning.
57. Tony has got a new watch.
58. Tony has a new watch.
59. We are just doing the homework.
60. You like Sally`s book.
61. You want to have the green pencil.
62. She buys some apples every day.
63. He is just reading a magazine.
64. Ann always goes to school at seven o`clock.
65. He never watches TV in the afternoon.
66. The children are paying for the hamburger.
67. You must dry the stamp.
68. She can have my book.
69. The children play in the playground every day.
70. We must do our homework.
71. She is looking for her keys.
72. He cannot buy the bread.
73. Tony always goes to school at seven.
74. We visit Uncle Mark in the summer holidays.
75. She washes her hair every day.
76. The dress is twelve pounds.
77. The train leaves at five pm.
78. Sally must look for her gloves.
79. Joe goes to bed, because he is ill.

QUESTIONS

1. Sue is running up the hill.
2. The bird is flying over the lake.
3. The dog likes to jump into the water.
4. They go to a party at Billy`s house.
5. Sally is sitting behind Tom.
6. It`s Maggie`s birthday.
7. Billy`s nose is red.
8. The boys go to the football match.
9. Pam throws a stone into the water.
10. The dog is holding a stick between its teeth.
11. Maggie has got a nice little dog.
12. The children want some sweets.
13. I`m good at playing tennis.
14. Trish likes ice-cream.
15. Billy is writing a letter after school.
16. Sam is a clever boy.
17. We buy some oranges.
18. I can do my homework alone.
19. She eats her lunch at twelve.
20. Mother shuts the window.
21. Father buys a new car.
22. We brush our teeth every morning.
23. The train leaves at nine pm.
24. Pat reads his book in bed.
25. There is a parcel for Maggie.
26. She draws a house.
27. I get a letter from Bob twice a month.
28. Sandy eats a sandwich, because he is hungry.
29. We must clean our room.
30. We must listen to the teacher.
31. He looks at my new dress.
32. She sews stars on her jeans.
33. He takes the present to his friend.
34. He helps me with the homework.
35. Trish goes to bed , because she is tired.
36. My new coat is beige.
37. The apples are one pound.
38. She likes my new jeans.
39. Mother buys a new pullover for Tom.

40. He calls me in the evening.
41. We don`t find Bill`s bike.
42. We may see the film.
43. Sandy must look for his keys.
44. He can eat two pizzas.
45. She wants a glass of beer.
46. He shows his work to the teacher.
47. Mr Miller buys six stamps for his letters.
48. The children can write a lot in English.
49. Sally has got nice photos.
50. Her grey sweater looks boring.
51. She wears her jeans skirt every day.
52. Your tights are too long.
53. Peter drinks hot chocolate in the morning.
54. He gets a present from his aunt.
55. Sally goes to bed, because it is late at night.
56. Mother always goes to market on Tuesday.
57. The baby is sleeping.
58. Pat usually has joghurt for breakfast.
59. Robert cannot find his socks.
60. Pit runs to school, because it is late.
61. The new coat is from Paris.
62. Mary stays with her granny.
63. This is mother's new hat.
64. Tom is sad, because there are no sweets for him.
65. Pam must look for her earrings.
66. The children eat all the cake.
67. Sue and Tom are swimming in the pond.
68. We prefer vanilla ice cream.
69. There is a nut tree in front of his house.
70. This is Ben's model car.
71. Father washes his car every week.
72. Charles eats two pizzas.
73. Fred always goes to school by bike.
74. Aunt Mary stays with the Coopers.
75. We like our Maths teacher.
76. Pam likes chocolate cake.
77. This is father's newspaper.
78. We have got a nice present for Phil.
79. She is working in the garden.
80. His car is a Ford.

UNCOUNTABLE WORDS

Für **unzählbare** Wörter verwendet man **some** oder man bedient sich verschiedener **Mengenangaben**.

some tea	or	**a cup of**	tea
		a glass of	tea
some water	or	**a bottle of**	water
		a glass of	water
		a basin of	water
		a litre of	water
		two litres of	water
some bread	or	**one pound of**	bread
		a piece of	bread
		a slice of (Schnitte)	bread
		a loaf of (Laib)	bread
		(two loaves of)	
some paper	or	**a piece of** (Stück)	paper
		a sheet of (Blatt)	paper
		a scrap of (Fetzen)	paper
			Attention: **a** paper = **a newspaper** (Zeitung)
some advice (Rat)	or	**a piece of**	advice
		a bit of	advice
some information	or	**a piece of**	information
		a bit of	information
		two bits of	information

ATTENTION:

glasses	**a pair of** glasses (Brille)	pyjamas	**a pair of** pyjamas
jeans	**a pair of** jeans	trousers	**a pair of** trousers
scales	**a pair of** scales (Waage)	pants	**a pair of** pants
compasses	**a pair of** compasses (Zirkel)	scissors	**a pair of** scissors

A AN SOME

SOME: 1) für Dinge im **Plural**, deren **genaue Menge** man nicht kennt.

2) für **unzählbare** Dinge.

1. Would you like .... coffee ? Yes, please.
2. Do you want .... apple ? No, thanks.
3. I`d like .... cornflakes, please.
4. Please, give me .... hamburger.
5. There is .... milk in the fridge.
6. We need .... eggs to bake a cake.
7. Is there .... orange juice left ? Yes, there is.
8. Take .... butter !
9. Would you like .... toast ?
10. There is .... egg on the floor !
11. I`d like .... roll and .... tea, please.
12. Please, buy .... oranges.
13. Please, get .... bread from the baker`s.
14. There is .... water in the basin.
15. I want to buy .... T-shirt and I need .... pullover, too.
16. Can I have .... coffee, please ?
17. You have got .... nice sticker album, Dave.
18. She invites .... boys and girls from her class.
19. Mum, I` ve got .... letter for you.
20. Mum, I`ve got .... letters for you.
21. There is .... open window. Please, shut it !
22. Jerry wants .... toast.
23. We watch TV on .... evenings of the week.
24. I need .... paper. I want to cut out .... paper animals.
25. I`d like to have .... piece of cake and .... tea.
26. I have got .... question.
27. I have got .... questions.
28. That`s .... good idea.
29. Let`s get .... grapes and .... cheese for dinner.
30. There is .... fly in the milk bottle.
31. Do you want .... ice cream, Bill ?
32. Bring .... bottles of wine, please.
33. I need .... money to buy .... presents.

34. Dad wants to have .... sugar for his coffee.
35. Here`s .... sausage for the dog.
36. Would you like .... more tea ?
37. Please, go and fetch .... onions from the garden.
38. I must buy .... milk at the dairy.
39. Have you got .... banana for me ?
Yes, there are .... in the basket.
40. I take .... cornflakes for breakfast.
41. I`d like .... egg, ... roll and .... orange juice, please.
42. Please, get me .... peanut butter and .... yoghurt.
43. Would you like .... more toast ?
44. Let's get .... grapes and .... cheese for our guests.
45. I'd like .... egg, please, ... boiled egg, ... roll and .... tea.
46. Mum, I've got .... flowers for you !
47. There's .... money on the kitchen table. Take it !
48. Please, give me .... advice.
49. Do you want .... bread ?
50. Do you need .... information ?
51 Would you like .... tea for breakfast ?
52 Can I have .... cheeseburger, please ?
53. Here's .... sausage for your dog. .... big sausage.
54. Would you like .... more sausages ? No, thanks.
55. I drink .... wine for lunch, Dad .... beer.
56. Do you like .... lemonade ?
57. What .... lovely birthday cake ! Can I have .... ?
58. Our neighbour has got .... red car.
59. Mum, I need .... new trousers !
60. Would you like .... chicken for lunch ?
61. I need .... information about hotels in Paris.
62. Ah, there's .... perfume in the air.
63. Fred needs .... new shoes. His old ones are too small.
64. Pit gets .... nice present for his birthday.
65. We need .... postcards and .... stamps.
66. Would you like .... cigarette ? No, thanks.
67. Fred and I are listening to .... good classical music.
68. Their garden is like a park with .... beautiful, old trees.
69. Go and fetch .... bottles of beer from the cellar, please.
70. There is .... water on the floor ! Don't slip !
71. Put .... honey on your bread !

THE POSSESSIVE CASE

1) is used for living beings

Singular	Plural
my brother' s book	my brothers' books
his sister' s ball	his two sisters' balls
Peter' s pen	my parents' house
Charles' s [-ziz] car	the Millers' house
James' s [-ziz] bike	the Coopers' party
Mr Miller' s house	the Smiths' son
Uncle Ben' s house	the boys' caps
at/to the baker' s (shop)	the girls' skirts
at the butcher' s	the Lincolns' pond
at the grocer' s	the twins' bikes
at the dentist' s	the Franklins' car
at the doctor' s	the Blackwells' dog
the cat' s name	the Fishers' guests
the child' s doll	the children' s dolls
the man' s coat	the men' s coats
the woman' s kitchen	the women' s hats

2) is used for

an hour' s walk	a two hours' walk
a minute' s walk	a three miles' ride
today' s paper	a four pounds' weight
yesterday' s news	a two minutes' call
a pound' s weight	an eight hours' sleep
a mile' s ride	a four weeks' holiday
a stone' s throw	a two weeks' trip

POSSESSIVE CASE

1. My brothers .... names are Rick and Jack.
2. What is your sister .... name ? - It is Susan.
3. My parents .... house is very nice.
4. This is St.James .... Palace.
5. Let's walk to St.Paul .... Cathedral.
6. It is only an hour .... walk.
7. What are your sisters .... names ?
8. After an hour .... ride we take a two hours .... rest.
9. Please, go to the baker .... and get some bread.
10. It's only a minute .... walk up the road.
11. Go and see the dentist .... .
12. This is a boy from Tim .... class.
13. The children .... shoes are dirty.
14. The dog .... name is Bello.
15. He likes his sister .... girlfriend.
16. The women .... coats are new.
17. It is only a stone .... throw from here.
18. What are your parents .... names ?
19. The Smiths .... house is big.
20. Mr Donald .... car is an Opel.
21. Where is yesterday .... newspaper ?
22. There is only today .... paper.
23. Frank .... bike is broken.
24. Mr Lampton .... garden is a park.
25. This is Bill from Sarah .... class.
26. Mandy .... birthday party is great.
27. Is it far ? - No, it is only half an hour .... walk from here.
28. These are my two brothers .... caps.
29. This is Keith .... bike at the door.
30. Mother is reading Joe .... letter.
31. I have got three weeks .... holiday.
32. Tom .... trousers are dirty.
33. The Carters .... car is red.
34. My sister .... room is tidy.
35. The children .... bikes are in the rain.
36. The baby needs ten hours .... sleep at night.
37. Mother is cooking for this evening .... dinner.
38. Mr Alan has got a week .... holiday.

THIS / THESE THAT / THOSE

For persons and things **near** the speaker we use **this** (singular)
these (plural)

For persons and things **farther away** we use **that** (singular)
those (plural)

Look, let`s buy **this** handbag. I like it.
These <u>here</u> are wonderful shoes !
This is Tom.- Hi, Tom !
I don`t like **those** apples <u>over there</u>.
Are **these** your books ? No, mine are **those** on the table <u>over there</u>.

Keep in mind:

this year	heuer
this morning	heute morgen
this time	diesmal

What`s **that** noise?	Was soll dieser Lärm?
Don`t do **that**.	Tu das nicht.
That`s all.	Das ist alles.
That`s that !	Erledigt!
That`ll do.	Das reicht.
At **that** time ...	Damals

THIS THAT THESE THOSE

1. Do you want .... apple here ?
2. I`d like to have .... book here, not .... book from the shelf.
3. Paul, ... is Peter.
4. Who is .... boy over there ?
5. .... is my friend Tom. - Hello Tom !
6. Please, give me .... glass from the shelf.
7. No, ... is my pen and .... pen over there is your pen !
8. Let`s buy .... pullover here.
9. Do you want .... cake here ?
10. Is .... my hat ? No, I think .... hat over there is yours.
11. .... pictures here are beautiful. - No, I prefer .... over there.
12. Look here ! In .... album there is a photo of my children.
13. The exercise on .... sheet is not very difficult.
14. Please, bring me .... vase over there.
15. .... woman near the door is Willy`s mum.
16. Do you like .... picture ?
17. Do you see .... house on the hill ?
18. .... presents are for you !
19. Thank you, ... flowers are nice !
20. Who are .... people in front of the garden ?
21. Excuse me, is .... your umbrella ?
22. Which dress do you like more ? .... or ....?
23. Which jeans do you prefer ? .... or ....?
24. I don`t know .... children near the door.
25. Are .... your cigarettes ?
26. Are .... your keys on the table over there ?
27. Oh, thanks ! .... is my handbag !
28. Excuse me, is .... seat free ?
29. Would you like .... apples or .... from behind ?
30. Who lives in .... house ? The Millers ? - No, they live in .... blue house at the end of the street.
31. How much are .... postcards ?
32. No, I`ll take ................... postcards over there. ....................`s all !
33. .... eggs are Easter eggs, but .... over there are not.
34. Look, there is a stain on ....trousers !
35. .... are my socks ! Your socks are .... over there.

36. Great ! .... film is with Sharon Stone !
37. I don`t like .... boring romantic films on TV.
38. Excuse me, is .... magazine free ?
39. Look at .... little boy high up in the tree !
40. Hi, are you Sally ? - No, Sally is .... girl on the terrace. I`m Liz.
41. I like .... hat, but .... hat there is not bad either (auch nicht schlecht).
42. .... morning it is not so cold.
43. Please, don`t do .... !
44. I hope summer will be fine ....year.
45. Let's buy .... hat here. It looks nice.
46. Sandy, ... is Mike. - Hello Mike !
47. Is .... my coat ? - No, I think .... coat over there is yours.
48. .... present is for you, Bill ! Happy birthday !
49. Are .... your cigarettes ? - No, I don't smoke.
50. .... is a nice dress, but it's very expensive. I think I'll take .... blue one over there. It is only 3o pounds.
51. Who lives in .... house here ? - Family Smith.
52. Excuse me, is .... menu free ? - Oh, of course ! Here you are !
53. How much are .... books ? They are 10 pounds each.
54. .... glasses are dirty.
55. .... glass is dirty. Take .... one over there.
56. Excuse me, is .... your car ? The lights are on.
57. .... are my tights ! Yours are ....over there !
58. Excuse me, is .... newspaper free ?
59. Thanks ! .... is my hat !
60. Give me .... blue bottle from the cupboard, please.
61. Hey, look, Frank ! .... is my new German teacher over there.
62. Do you like .... apples here ? - No, thanks , I prefer .... red ones over there.
63. I hate .... horror films on TV.
64. Look, ... aeroplane is very high up in the sky.
65. .... flowers are for you, Mum.
66. I don' t like .... hamburger. It is too salty.
67. I like .... photo here very much.
68. Do you see .... tree on the hill ? It’s a hundred years old.
69. Let's buy .... book here for his birthday.
70. Please, bring me .... jar from the shelf.

WORD ORDER

Time	Subject	Predicate	Object	Place	Time
Every day	Jill	reads	a book	in her room	in the evening.

Attention: always, usually, often, sometimes, rarely, seldom, ever, never, also, just, still, already, both, all **must be placed**

1) **before** the verb : I **always go** to work by car.
She **never does** her homework in the evening.
We **rarely watch** TV.
She **often has** tea for breakfast.

2) **after :** is , am , are, was, were, can, may, must, will , would

I **am never** ill.
They **are usually** at home in the evening.
She **can never** do her homework alone.
He **will always** remember you.
She **would never** do that !

3) **between:** have ......got, have ....been

I **have never been** to Rome.
I **have often got** muesli for breakfast.
They **have all got** the flu.

4) **before:** have to

I **often have to** work too much.
He **never has to** help in the kitchen.

If there are **two time expressions**, the **more detailed** comes **first.**

We eat **at one o`clock on Monday.**
He `ll arrive **at 11 h tomorrow morning.**

WORD ORDER

1. a newspaper / reads / every day / Jill.
2. football / don`t like / very much / I.
3. always / forget / watch / my / I / in the morning / in the bathroom.
4. every day / do / the same thing / we.
5. I / this picture / don`t like / very much.
6. in her handbag / mother / puts / in the morning / her money.
7. two cigarettes / she / every day / before breakfast / smokes.
8. at the concert / meet / we / some friends / this evening.
9. He / the same clothes / every day / does not / wear.
10. to work / every morning / walks / George.
11. at the party / we / arrive / early in the evening.
12. to bed / I / usually / go / early / in the evening.
13. goes / every year / to Italy / Tom / in summer.
14. I / in bed / my breakfast / have / in the morning.
15. in October / Barbara / to University / will go.
16. always / in the bus / forget / I / my umbrella / in the morning.
17. she / all evening / TV / watches.
18. a lot of people / to the party / we / invite / today evening.
19. was / a great / birthday party / yesterday / it.
20. to me / my neighbour / never / speaks.
21. polite / is / Susan / always.
22. finish / work / I / at half past ten / every night.
23. rarely / she / to bed / goes / before midnight.
24. he / often / does not / meat / eat.
25. I / remember / can / his name / never.
26. is / late / the / usually / bus / not.
27. in bed / he / is / still.
28. ill / never / he / is .
29. often / very cold / is / in winter / here / it .
30. you / for breakfast / usually / have / do / what ?
31. she / tired / always / is / in the evening.
32. you / do / often / in restaurants / eat ?
33. sometimes / too much / I / eat.
34. to work / he / goes/ always / in the morning / by car.
35. plays / tennis / often / in the afternoon / Pit.
36. feels / sad / she / sometimes.
37. Bob / is / never / sad .
38. at seven o`clock / they / usually / have / dinner / in the evening.

39. in / London / they / all / live.
40. Pit / plays / also / football and basketball / two times a week.
41. brothers / my / both / are / doctors.
42. I / always / remember / you / will.
43. usually / go / you / do / by bus / home / after school ?
44. I / never / can / find / my / keys / when I come home.
45. in summer / rarely / snows / it.
46. must / he / always / do / in the afternoon / his homework.
47. she / tomorrow evening / will arrive / at seven o`clock.
48. goes / Ann / to school / every day.
49. eat / in the morning / bananas / often / they.
50. a headache / never / Sandy / has.
51. at McDonald`s / often / buy / the children / a hamburger.
52. wears / to school / jeans / Ann / often.
53. cannot eat / Arnold / all / things / the / nice.
54. is / Cindy / at home / not / at school / but / is / she.
55. just / Peter / having / his breakfast / is .
56. like / you / do / apples ?
57. to music / your / listening / brother / is.
58. usually / have / breakfast / when / do / in / morning / the / you?
59. in front of / the cat / standing / the / is / mousehole / it / see / doesn`t / but / a / mouse .
60. go / school / to / time / what / you / do / day / every ?
61. often / meets / his friends / Tony / at 4 pm. / in the park.
62. good / what / are / you / at ?
63. skiing / at / I / good / am / but / skating / like / don`t / I .
64. often / Mandy / to her penfriend / writes / a postcard / in England.
65. English / the children / like to speak / at school.
66. Pat's room / full of / animals / is / posters of .
67. loves / my mother / but / I / romantic films / hate / them.
68. in the playground / every day / the boys / play.
69. must / children / hamburger / pay / the / for / the .
70. Tony / got / a / watch / new / has / for / birthday / his.
71. green / pencil / I / have / to / want / the / please.
72. on Monday / eat / we / at twelve o'clock.
73. are / usually / they / in the evening / at home.
74. Bob / ill / is / never / in winter.
75. TV / rarely / watch / we / in the afternoon.
76. present / the / takes / his / friend / Bob / to.
77. the teacher / to / he / shows / his homework / in the morning.

PAST TENSE

We use the past tense for actions that happened :

yesterday
last week (month, year)
in 1982 ....
in September (last year ....)
on Monday (last week ....)
at five o`clock ....
ago
before

1) regular verbs: add - ed

stay - stayed	stud**y** - stud**ied**
like - liked	marr**y** - marr**ied**
work - worked	pla**n** - pla**nn**ed
play - played	sto**p** - sto**pp**ed

2) irregular verbs: you must learn them by heart (see list!)

go - went	say - said
do - did	have - had
take - took	be - was / were
run - ran	can - could

Attention: I **was**
You **were**
he, she, it **was**
we, you, they **were**

Examples: Yesterday I **went** to school at seven o`clock.
She **was** in Italy in 1995.
We **had** breakfast at eight.

Question and negation in past tense:

1) with did / didn`t:

Did you **go** to school yesterday ? No, I **didn`t go** because I was ill.
Did you **see** George in town ? No, we **didn`t see** him.
Why **did** he **not come** ? He **didn`t hear** the phone !
When **did** he **arrive** ? He **didn`t arrive**.
Did you **find** your keys ? No, I **didn`t find** them.

2) without did / didn`t: was, were, could,
questions with **who /1.Fall**

Were you tired yesterday evening ? No, I **wasn `t.**
Was she at home last night ? No, she **wasn`t**. She was at Peter's.
Was he ill last week ? No, he **wasn`t.**
Who was in the cinema ? Tom? No, Tom **wasn`t** in the cinema.
Could you **do** your homework alone ? No, I **couldn`t**. Father helped.

LIST OF THE MOST IMPORTANT IRREGULAR VERBS

be	was
blow	blew
buy	bought
come	came
do	did
drive	drove
feed	fed
forget	forgot
go	went
hear	heard
hold	held
know	knew
let	let
make	made
put	put
ring	rang
say	said
send	sent
steal	stole
shut	shut
sleep	slept
stand	stood
tell	told
throw	threw
weep	wept

begin	began
break	broke
can	could
cut	cut
draw	drew
eat	ate
find	found
get	got
grow	grew
hide	hid
hurt	hurt
lead	led
lie	lay
meet	met
read [i:]	read [e]
rise	rose
see	saw
set	set
shine	shone
sing	sang
speak	spoke
swim	swam
teach	taught
wake	woke
win	won

bind	bound
build	built
catch	caught
dig	dug
drink	drank
fall	fell
fly	flew
give	gave
have	had
hit	hit
keep	kept
leave	left
lose	lost
pay	paid
ride	rode
run	ran
sell	sold
shake	shook
shoot	shot
sit	sat
spend	spent
take	took
think	thought
wear	wore
write	wrote

PRESENT TENSE OR PAST TENSE

1. Last year she .... 22, so she .... 23 now. (be)
2. Today the weather .... nice, but yesterday it .... cold. (be)
3. I .... hungry now. (be)
4. He .... (be) hungry last night, so I .... (give) him something to eat.
5. Where .... (you / be) at 11 o`clock last Friday ?
6. Don`t buy these shoes. They .... (be) too expensive.
7. Why ....you (be) so angry yesterday ?
8. We must go now. It .... (be) very late.
9. This time last year I .... (be) in Paris.
10. We .... (be) tired when we .... (arrive) yesterday.
11. We .... (go) to bed at ten yesterday.
12. Charlie Caplin .... (be) a famous film star.
13. Where .... (be) the children ? I don`t know.
    They .... (be) in the garden ten minutes ago.
14. We .... (not like) our hotel last year. It .... (be) small and it .... (not be) very clean.
15. I .... (phone) you yesterday evening, but you .... (not be) at home.
16. He .... (not / be) at work last week, because he .... (be) ill. But he .... (be) much better now.
17. The shops .... (be) open yesterday.
18. .... (you / be) at home yesterday?
    No, I .... (not / be) , I .... (be) at work.
19. I .... (see) an interesting film last night.
20. .... (you / watch) the film yesterday ?
    I never .... (watch) TV.
21. I .... (go) to a museum last week.
    It .... (be) great ! I .... (like) it very much.
22. He .... (be) tired now.
    I .... (be) tired yesterday evening.
23. The weather .... (be) warm yesterday.
24. When I .... (be) a child I .... (be) afraid of dogs.
25. Where .... (you / be) yesterday at three o`clock ?
26. These shoes .... (be) nice.
    Where .... (you / buy) them ?
27. Why .... (he / be) so happy yesterday ?
28. We .... (have) a nice time last holidays.

PAST TENSE QUESTIONS

1. Peter was angry.
2. Bob went to his friend.
3. Simon asked Sally for help.
4. Our grandparents came at Christmas.
5. The monkey hid his banana in the tree.
6. Peter looked for his keys.
7. They could not find their books.
8. Bob watched the late-night film.
9. Mother poured milk into my glass.
10. She sewed a new dress.
11. They sat in front of our house.
12. The car parked near our house.
13. They had to run to school, because they missed the bus.
14. Sandy ate my hot dog.
15. Bill was not good at climbing trees.
16. Pam wanted to have a baby doll.
17. She could not do her homework alone.
18. We had to look for Marc.
19. Tom wanted to climb the high tree.
20. The children went to a birthday party.
21. Maggie helped her mother in the kitchen.
22. His schoolbag was green.
23. Mr Simons lived in London.
24. Peter went to bed, because he felt tired.
25. The dog ran after the cat.
26. We visited Aunt Mary in our holidays.
27. We did a lot of work last week.
28. The plane left at three in the morning.
29. She waited for her friend.
30. He got a toy car from Uncle Marc.
31. Their uniforms were blue.
32. Ann listened to cassettes in bed.
33. The dress was 34 pounds.
34. Mum sewed a dark blue dress for Susan.
35. Charles ate two pizzas !
36. He got a good mark in English.
37. They looked at the photos in their album.
38. We liked Mr Manson very much.

PAST TENSE QUESTIONS

39. Sandy ate three slices of cake.
40. This was Phil's old cap.
41. He always went to work by bus.
42. We met Robert in the park.
43. He did his homework at three pm.
44. He cleaned his shoes twice a week.
45. They went to church on Sundays.
46. They lived in Paris.
47. Bob came in the evening.
48. He came from Windsor.
49. Paul went skiing on Friday.
50. Susan wrote a letter to her penfriend.
51. Father brought a present for Tom.
52. Mum bought warm tights for Susan.
53. Pit rode his bike in the afternoon.
54. We had to clean our rooms.
55. They made a trip to Greece.
56. I got a letter from my friend in Paris.
57. We bought some oranges at the market.
58. We looked at the new photos.
59. He took the present to his friend.
60. Pit read his book in the afternoon.
61. Paul called me from Switzerland in the evening.
62. It was Mary's birthday.
63. Mother shut the window, because it was cold.
64. My old coat was grey.
65. Mother made a plan for the week.
66. We cooked spaghetti.
67. She said 'Hello' to us.
68. Pat told us the truth.
69. We went by taxi.
70. A big stone hit their car.
71. The children hid behind the bushes.
72. Mary sang a lovely song.
73. Dad took us to Paris.
74. They shook hands.
75. The bell rang at twelve o'clock.

GOING TO FUTURE

wird verwendet wenn du etwas planst oder zu tun beabsichtigst:

I	**am going to**	write a letter.
You	**are going to**	help father.
He	**is going to**	make a trip.
She	**is going to**	spend her holidays in Italy.
It	**is going to**	eat its bone.
We	**are going to**	bake a cake.
You	**are going to**	buy a big house.
They	**are going to**	make a trip to France.

QUESTIONS:

Where **are you going to** spend your holidays ?
Are you going to have a party ?
Is he going to buy a new car ?
Is she going to invite her friends ?
Are they going to paint their room ?
Are we going to go to Paris ?

PRESENT TENSE SIMPLE, PROGRESSIVE, GOING TO FUTURE, PAST TENSE

1. .... (you / be) at the party last Friday ? No, I .... (not be), I .... (have) a bad cold and I .... (must) stay in bed.
2. We .... (go) to Italy in our next holidays.
3. They .... (spend) their last holidays at the sea. They .... (have) a lot of fun. They .... (go) swimming every day and they .... (eat) lots of ice cream and they .... (play) in the sand and they all .... (be) happy.
4. She .... (not see) the interesting news last night. What a pity!
5. He .... (go) to bed at ten at night. I .... (think) that .... (be) too late for him.
6. Listen ! The baby .... (cry) !
7. Uncle Jim .... (be) in hospital last week, because he .... (break) his leg.
8. What .... (you / do) this afternoon ? Oh, I .... (ride) my bike.
9. .... (you / listen to) the news yesterday evening ? No, I .... (not / have) any time. I .... (must) do my homework.
10. He usually .... (drink) orange juice in the morning, but today he .... (drink) a glass of milk.
11. Where .... (be) Susan and Tom? - They .... (be) in the garden some minutes ago. - Oh, yes, look ! They .... (hide) behind a tree !
12. He .... (call) me yesterday evening. It .... (be) very late.
13. In a few minutes there .... (be) a heavy thunderstorm.
14. He .... (not / can) go to school last week, because he .... (be) ill.
15. Hello Tim ! I .... (have) a party next week. - Oh, that`s fine !
16. The shops .... (be) closed yesterday. They .... (be) always closed on Sundays.
17. I never.......................... (watch) late night films on TV, because I .... (must go) to bed at eight.

18. Sally ! What .... (you / do) at the moment ? -
Oh, nothing special ! I .... (write) an invitation card for my party. .... (you / need) me ?
19. Who .... (come) to your party next week ?
20. Saron Stone .... (be) a famous film star.
I .... (like) her .
21. Look at greedy Oliver ! He .... (put) toffees into his mouth by the fistful.
22. Normally she .... (sleep) very long in the holidays, but this morning she .... (not / can) sleep any longer because the baby .... (cry). Poor Sally !
23. .... (you / like) your new classmates ? Yes, they all .... (be) very nice and helpful.
24. What .... (you / do) with the knife ? -
I .... (cut) some bread.
25. Ben, you .... (eat up) all my sweets yesterday !
26. He .... (go) away yesterday without saying a word.
27. An hour ago she .... (buy) a nice dress.
It .... (not / be) cheap !
28. We rarely .... (watch) TV at night.
29. Bob .... (buy) a bike tomorrow.
30. She usually .... (have) her recorder lesson on Monday, but last week it .... (be) on Tuesday.
31. Sue .... (write) a letter to her penfriend tomorrow.
32. She .... (set) the table for dinner a few minutes ago. She always .... (set) the table for dinner.
33. Last month granny .... (bring) some lovely presents.
She always .... (have) nice presents for us.
34. .... (you / hear) that strange noise last night ? –
No, I .... (not / hear) it !
35. On Friday mother usually .... (go) shopping, but last Friday she .... (go) to the cinema, because there .... (be) a film with Tom Hanks.
36. Ann .... (sleep) very well last night, so she .... (not / hear) that strange noise.
37. I .... (meet) him last week.
He .... (be) fresh and healthy.
38. Where .... (you / build) your new house next year ? -
We .... (still look for) some nice place.
39. Look out of the window ! It ....(snow) !

QUESTIONS : PRESENT SIMPLE , PROGRESSIVE PAST TENSE , GOING TO FUTURE

1. Last night the children were very tired.
2. Sandy ate bread and butter.
3. He is going to come tomorrow.
4. Mary is singing a funny song.
5. Fred didn't go to school, because he was ill.
6. They go to a restaurant on Sundays.
7. They had chicken for dinner.
8. Grandfather sleeps after lunch.
9. Liz and her sister are going to spend their holidays in Greece.
10. He likes cornflakes for breakfast.
11. They often went to the cinema last year.
12. They are cutting out paper butterflies.
13. Uncle Marc visited us last Saturday.
14. We sometimes go skiing in winter.
15. They are drinking a cup of coffee now.
16. Pam is going to bake a cake for the weekend.
17. The concert begins at eight pm..
18. The Fishers are going to make a trip to Saalbach.
19. They have got a flat there.
20. The children are playing basketball.
21. We travelled by plane last summer.
22. Sally has got a new bike.
23. The trousers were 20 pounds.
24. He has got 250 different stamps.
25. Last week we saw Keith in Salzburg.
25. Mum is going to invite some friends.
27. In 1997 Peter won the downhill race in Saalbach.
28. Tom is Susan's brother.
29. Dad is working at our pond.
30. He is fishing leaves.
31. Mike and Ann went to the cinema two weeks ago.
32. Mother never plays football.
33. Rick has got toothache.
34. Brenda said nothing to Tim.
35. Our children usually go to bed at eight.

WORDS

a bad cold	*starke Verkühlung*	between	*zwischen*
a bit of	*ein wenig, etwas*	bicycle,bike	*Fahrrad*
a cold	*eine Erkältung*	bird	*Vogel*
a lot of	*viel*	biro	*Kugelschreiber*
accident	*Unfall*	birthday	*Geburtstag*
advice	*Rat*	bite	*beißen, Biss*
afraid of	*fürchten vor*	blouse	*Bluse*
after	*nach*	blow	*blasen*
afternoon	*Nachmittag*	board	*Tafel*
again and again	*immer wieder*	boiled	*gekocht*
ago	*vor*	bone	*Knochen*
air	*Luft*	boring	*langweilig*
airport	*Flugplatz*	bottle	*Flasche*
all	*alle,alles*	box	*Schachtel,Box*
alone	*allein*	bread	*Brot*
alright	*in Ordnung*	break	*brechen*
always	*immer*	breakfast	*Frühstück*
angry	*zornig*	brother	*Bruder*
animal	*Tier*	brush	*Bürste,bürsten*
another	*ein anderes,anderer*	build	*bauen*
arrive	*ankommen*	bush	*Busch*
arrogant	*arrogant*	busstop	*Bushaltestelle*
as a rule	*in der Regel*	butcher	*Fleischhauer*
ask	*fragen*	butterfly	*Schmetterling*
at home	*zu Hause*	buy	*kaufen*
at present	*nun, jetzt*	by car	*mit dem Auto*
at the moment	*im Augenblick*	by the fistful	*Handvoll*
atlas	*Atlas*	cake	*Kuchen*
aunt	*Tante*	calf	*Kalb;Wade*
awful	*schrecklich*	call	*rufen,anrufen,Anruf*
bag	*Tasche*	can	*können*
bake	*backen*	castle	*Schloss*
bark	*bellen*	cat	*Katze*
basin	*Waschbecken*	catch	*fangen*
basket	*Korb*	caterpillar	*Raupe*
bathroom	*Badezimmer*	cellar	*Keller*
beautiful	*schön*	chair	*Sessel*
because	*weil*	chat	*Gespräch,Plauderei*
bed	*Bett*	cheese	*Käse*
beer	*Bier*	chewing gum	*Kaugummi*
before	*vor* (zeitlich)	chicken	*Huhn*
beginning	*Beginn*	chief	*Häuptling,Chef*
behind	*hinter*	children	*Kinder*
beige	*beige,hellbraun*	Christmas carol	*Weihnachtslied*
bend	*beugen*	city	*Stadt*
berry	*Beere*	classmate	*Klassenkamerad*
best	*am besten,das Beste*	clean	*sauber,rein;reinigen*
better than	*besser als*	clever	*klug*

cliff	*Klippe*	egg	*Ei*
climb	*klettern*	empty	*leer*
close	*schließen*	European	*europäisch*
coat	*Mantel*	every	*jeder,jede,jedes*
cold	*kalt,Erkältung*	everything	*alles*
collection	*Sammlung*	exam	*Prüfung*
colour	*Farbe*	example	*Beispiel*
comb	*Kamm,kämmen*	excuse me	*Entschuldigung*
compass	*Kompass*	exercises	*Übungen,Turnüb.*
cook	*kochen,Koch*	expect	*erwarten*
correct	*richtig;korrigieren*	expensive	*teuer*
could you	*könntest/konntest du*	eye	*Auge*
cow	*Kuh*	face	*Gesicht*
crazy	*verrückt*	fall	*fallen*
cry	*weinen,schreien*	famous	*berühmt*
cup	*Tasse*	far	*weit*
cupboard	*Schrank*	farther away	*weiter weg*
curtain	*Vorhang*	fast	*schnell*
cut	*schneiden*	favourite	*Lieblings-*
dairy	*Molkerei*	feed	*füttern*
dance	*tanzen,Tanz*	feel	*fühlen*
dark green	*dunkelgrün*	feet	*Füße*
dead	*tot*	felt-tip	*Filzstift*
deer	*Hirsch,Damwild*	fetch	*holen,bringen*
dentist	*Zahnarzt*	find	*finden*
desire	*wünschen, sehnen*	fine	*fein*
detailed	*ausführlich,genau*	finish	*beenden*
die	*sterben*	first	*erster,erste,erstes*
difficult	*schwierig*	fish	*Fisch,fischen*
dig	*graben*	flat	*flach,Wohnung*
dinner	*Abendessen*	flavour	*Geschmacksrichtung*
dirty	*schmutzig*	floor	*Fußboden,Stockwerk*
dislike	*nicht mögen*	flower	*Blume*
disturb	*stören*	flu	*Grippe*
dog	*Hund*	fly	*Fliege,fliegen*
doll	*Puppe*	food	*Essen*
downhill race	*Schirennen*	foot	*Fuß*
draw	*zeichnen*	for joy	*vor Freude*
dream	*träumen*	forget	*vergessen*
dress	*Kleid*	fox	*Fuchs*
drive	*fahren,lenken*	France	*Frankreich*
drop	*tropfen;fallen lassen*	free	*frei*
dry	*trocken,trocknen*	French	*französisch*
duster	*Staubtuch*	fresh	*frisch*
ear	*Ohr*	fridge	*Kühlschrank*
early	*früh*	friend	*Freund*
earring	*Ohrring*	friendly	*freundlich*
Easter	*Ostern*	frog	*Frosch*
easy	*leicht*	fruit	*Obst,Frucht*
eat	*essen*	fruit gum	*Fruchtgummi*

full of	*voll von*	hurry	*Eile,beeilen*
fun	*Spaß*	hurt	*Verletzung,verletzen*
funny	*lustig*	idea	*Idee*
game	*Spiel*	ill	*krank*
gate	*Gartentür,Tor*	in front of	*vor (örtlich)*
geese	*Gänse*	inch	*2,54cm*
generally	*für gewöhnlich*	interesting	*interessant*
gentleman	*Herr*	invitation card	*Einladungskarte*
girlfriend	*Freundin*	invite	*einladen*
give	*geben*	iron	*bügeln*
glass	*Glas*	island	*Insel*
glasses	*Brillen*	Italian	*italienisch*
gloves	*Handschuhe*	jacket	*Jacke*
go well with	*gut passen zu*	jar	*Glas,Krug*
go with	*passen zu*	juice	*Saft*
goose	*Gans*	jump	*hüpfen*
granny	*Oma*	just	*gerade*
grape	*Weintraube*	keep	*halten,behalten*
grass	*Gras*	key	*Schlüssel*
great	*großartig,toll*	kiss	*Kuss,küssen*
Greece	*Griechenland*	kitchen	*Küche*
grocer	*Kaufmann*	kite	*Papierdrachen*
grow	*wachsen*	knee	*Knie*
guest	*Gast*	knife	*Messer*
guitar	*Gitarre*	know	*wissen,kennen*
hair	*Haar*	lady	*Dame*
hamster	*Hamster*	lake	*See*
hand out	*austeilen*	late	*spät*
handbag	*Handtasche*	lazy	*faul*
handkerchief	*Taschentuch*	lead	*führen*
hanky	*Taschentuch*	leaf	*Blatt*
happy	*glücklich*	leaves	*Blätter*
hat	*Hut*	lemon	*Zitrone*
hate	*hassen*	let	*lassen*
have a cold	*verkühlt sein*	letter	*Brief*
headache	*Kopfweh*	lice	*Läuse*
healthy	*gesund*	lie	*liegen,lügen*
heavy	*schwer*	life	*Leben*
help,helpful	*Hilfe,hilfsbereit*	light	*Licht*
here you are	*da hast du*	like	*gern haben*
hill	*Hügel*	listen	*zuhören*
hit	*schlagen*	litre	*Liter*
hold	*halten*	little	*klein,wenig*
holiday	*Ferien*	living room	*Wohnzimmer*
honey	*Honig*	loaf	*Brotlaib*
hop	*hüpfen*	loaves	*Laibe*
hope	*hoffen*	locker	*Kasten*
hot	*heiß*	lolly	*Lutscher*
hour	*Stunde*	look at	*ansehen*
hungry	*hungrig*	look for	*suchen*

look forward to	*sich freuen auf*
lose	*verlieren*
loud	*laut*
love	*lieben*
lovely	*nett,lieb,gut*
lunch	*Mittagessen*
magazine	*Zeitschrift*
make	*Automarke,machen*
many	*viele*
mark	*Note*
marry	*heiraten*
match	*passen,Streichholz*
may	*dürfen*
meal	*Mahl*
mean	*bedeuten*
meet	*treffen*
menu	*Speisekarte*
mice	*Mäuse*
midnight	*Mitternacht*
mile	*Meile*
minerals	*Mineralien*
miss	*versäumen,-missen*
model car	*Modellauto*
model plane	*Modellflugzeug*
money	*Geld*
monkey	*Affe*
mouse	*Maus*
mouth	*Mund*
move	*bewegen*
muesli	*Müsli*
must	*müssen*
nationality	*Nationalität*
near	*nahe*
need	*brauchen*
neighbour	*Nachbar*
nest	*Nest*
never	*nie*
new	*neu*
newspaper	*Zeitung*
nice	*nett*
night	*Nacht*
noise	*Lärm*
normally	*normalerweise*
nose	*Nase*
nothing special	*nichts Besonderes*
now	*nun,jetzt*
nut tree	*Nussbaum*
of course	*natürlich*
office	*Büro*
once	*einmal,einst*
onion	*Zwiebel*
open	*öffnen,offen*
order	*bestellen*
ordinary	*gewöhnlich*
outside	*draußen*
over	*über,vorüber*
over there	*dort drüben*
ox	*Ochse*
oxen	*Ochsen*
paint	*malen*
painter	*Maler*
pants	*kurzeHose*
parcel	*Paket*
parents	*Eltern*
parrot	*Papagei*
pass	*vorbeigehen*
paw	*Pfote*
pay	*bezahlen*
pencil	*Bleistift*
penguin	*Pinguin*
penfriend,penpal	*Brieffreund*
perfume	*Parfum*
pet	*Haustier*
phone	*anrufen,Telefon*
piano	*Klavier*
piano lesson	*Klavierstunde*
picture	*Bild*
piece	*Stück*
plan	*Plan*
plane	*Flugzeug*
play	*spielen*
play catch	*Fangen spielen*
playground	*Spielplatz*
play hide and seek	*Verstecken spielen*
pocket	*Tasche (der Hose)*
pocket calculator	*Taschenrechner*
poem	*Gedicht*
point at	*zeigen auf*
policeman	*Polizist*
polite	*höflich*
pond	*Teich*
poor	*arm*
post office	*Postamt*
postcard	*Postkarte*
pot plant	*Blumenstock*
potato	*Kartoffel*
pour	*eingießen*
prepare	*bereiten,herrichten*
present	*Geschenk*
price	*Preis,Kosten*

pupil	*Schüler*
put	*setzen,stellen,legen*
question	*Frage,fragen*
quiet	*ruhig*
rabbit	*Kaninchen*
rain	*Regen*
raise	*erheben,hochheben*
rarely	*selten*
rat	*Ratte*
read	*lesen*
ready	*fertig*
recognize	*wiedererkennen*
record	*Schallplatte*
recorder	*Flöte,Rekorder*
remember	*sich erinnern*
rest	*Ruhe,ausruhen;Rest*
rich	*reich*
ride	*reiten*
right	*richtig,rechts*
ring	*Ring*
rise	*sich erheben*
river	*Fluss*
rock	*Felsen*
roll	*Semmel*
rose	*Rose*
rubber	*Radiergummi*
sad	*traurig*
salty	*salzig*
satchel	*Schultasche*
sausage	*Wurst*
say	*sagen*
scales	*Waage*
scissors	*Schere*
scrap of paper	*Fetzen Papier*
sea	*Meer*
seat	*Sitz,Platz*
seldom	*selten*
sell	*verkaufen*
send	*senden*
set	*Tisch decken;stellen*
sew	*nähen*
shake	*schütteln*
sharp	*scharf*
sharpener	*Spitzer*
sheep	*Schaf*
sheet of paper	*Blatt Papier*
shelf	*Regal*
shine	*scheinen*
shirt	*Hemd*
shoes	*Schuhe*
shoot	*schießen*
shop	*Geschäft,einkaufen*
shopping	*Einkaufen*
short	*klein,kurz*
shout	*schreien,rufen*
shower	*Dusche*
shut	*schließen*
sister	*Schwester*
sit	*sitzen*
skate	*eislaufen*
skirt	*Mädchenrock*
sleep	*schlafen,Schlaf*
sleepy	*schläfrig*
slice	*Schnitte*
slip	*ausrutschen*
small	*klein*
smell	*riechen,Duft,Geruch*
smoke	*rauchen,Rauch*
snake	*Schlange*
socks	*Socken*
sofa	*Sofa*
something	*etwas*
sorry	*Entschuldigung*
speak	*sprechen*
spearmint	*grüne Minze*
spell	*buchstabieren*
spider	*Spinne*
spinach	*Spinat*
stain	*Fleck*
stamp	*stampfen,Marke*
star	*Stern*
station	*Bahnhof*
stay	*bleiben*
stay with	*bleiben bei*
steal	*stehlen*
steep	*steil*
sticker album	*Pickerlheft*
still	*noch*
stomachache	*Magenschmerzen*
stone	*Stein*
story	*Geschichte*
strange	*seltsam*
strawberries	*Erdbeeren*
strong	*stark*
study	*lernen*
sugar	*Zucker*
suit	*passen*
sweet	*Süßigkeit,süß*
Switzerland	*Schweiz*
tail	*Schwanz*

take	*nehmen*	ugly	*hässlich*
tall	*groß*	grey	*grau*
tape recorder	*Tonbandgerät*	umbrella	*Regenschirm*
tasty	*schmackhaft*	uncle	*Onkel*
tea	*Tee*	under	*unter*
teach	*lehren*	understand	*verstehen*
teeth	*Zähne*	unhappy	*unglücklich*
tell	*erzählen*	uniform	*Uniform*
terrible	*schrecklich*	unit	*Lektion*
test	*Schularbeit,testen*	useful	*nützlich*
thanks	*danke*	usually	*für gewöhnlich*
the same thing	*dasselbe*	very much	*sehr(viel)*
thief	*Dieb*	visit	*besuchen*
thin	*dünn*	wait for	*warten auf*
think	*denken*	wake up	*aufwachen,-wecken*
thirsty	*durstig*	walk	*(spazieren)gehen*
three times	*dreimal*	wash	*waschen*
throw	*Wurf,werfen*	watch	*ansehen*
thunderstorm	*Gewitter*	way	*Weg*
ticket	*Eintrittskarte*	wear	*tragen(Kleidung)*
tie	*Krawatte*	week	*Woche*
tights	*Strumpfhose*	weekend	*Wochenende*
time	*Zeit*	weep	*weinen*
tin	*Konservendose*	weight	*Gewicht*
tired	*müde*	what a pity	*wie schade*
today	*heute*	what kind of	*was für ein,eine*
toe	*Zehe*	whenever	*immer wenn*
toffee	*Stolwerk*	where	*wo*
together	*gemeinsam*	who	*wer*
tomato	*Tomate*	whose	*wessen*
too big	*zu groß*	wife	*Ehefrau*
tooth	*Zahn*	will	*werden*
toothbrush	*Zahnbürste*	win	*gewinnen*
touch	*berühren*	window	*Fenster*
town	*Stadt*	wine	*Wein*
toy	*Spielzeug*	wipe off	*abwischen*
train	*Zug*	wish	*Wunsch, wünschen*
trainers	*Turnschuhe*	with	*mit*
tree	*Baum*	wolf	*Wolf*
trip	*Reise*	woman	*Frau*
trousers	*Hose*	wonderful	*wunderbar*
truth	*Wahrheit*	would	*würde*
try	*probieren*	wrong	*falsch*
try on	*anprobieren*	yesterday	*gestern*
turn around	*herumdrehen*	young	*jung*
turn off	*abdrehen*		
turn on	*aufdrehen*		
twice	*zweimal*		
twins	*Zwillinge*		
tyre	*Reifen*		

NAMES

Girls	Boys
Ann	Alan
Betty	Barry
Brenda	Basil
Carol	Ben
Cathy	Bill
Cindy	Billy
Clare	Bob
Daisy	Brian
Eve	Charles
Jill	Col(l)in
Lisa	Dean
Lynn	Eric
Maggie	Franc
Mandy	Fred
Mary	Jeff
Milly	Jerry
Molly	Jim
Nancy	Jimmy
Nelly	Joe
Nora	John
Olivia	Ken
Pam	Marc
Pamela	Mick
Pat	Pat
Sally	Patrick
Sandra	Phil
Sandy	Pit
Sarah	Rick
Sharon	Roger
Sheila	Sam
Shirley	Sandy
Stella	Simon
Sue	Tim
Susan	Tom
Tina	Tony
Tracy	William
Trish	Willie

KEY

pages 2,3

1. **an** ice cream
2. **a** name for **a** boy or **a** girl
3. **an** exercise book and **a** good pen
4. **a** rubber
5. **an** English name
6. **a** very good boy
7. **an** English book
8. **a** new English book
9. **a** radio programme
10. **an** orange
11. **a** brother
12. **an** orange cat.
13. **a** blue
14. **an** exercise book
15. **an** apple
16. **an** old schoolbag
17. **an** old teacher
18. **an** English car
19. **an** Austrian boy
20. **an** English boy
21. **an** American girl
22. **an** orange
23. **a** handbag
24. **an** old T-shirt
25. **an** English, **an** Austrian
26. **an** apple
27. **an** ice cream
28. **a** hamburger
29. **a** boiled egg, **an** egg
30. **an** orange pullover
31. **a** cheese sandwich
32. **an** empty glass
33. **an** atlas
34. **an** aunt
35. **an** English book
36. **an** American boy
37. **a** lolly
38. **a** pink felt-tip
39. **a** blue satchel , **a** brown
40. **an** umbrella, **an** orange
41. **a** blue umbrella
42. **an** earring
43. **a** banana
44. **a** good breakfast
45. **an** animal
46. **a** nice animal
47. **a** nice uniform
48. **an** uncle
49. **an** easy exercise
50. **an** orange and **a** banana
51. **a** hamburger or **a** hot dog
52. **a** nice pet
53. **an** expensive car
54. **a** hat
55. **a** good idea
56. **a** nice animal
57. **a** lolly
58. **an** orange floor
59. **a** party
60. **a** party, **a** great idea
61. **a** new song
62. **a** big orange
63. **an** orange
64. **a** new T-shirt
65. **a** book
66. **a** grey cat
67. **a** headache
68. **a** snack bar
69. **a** hot dog
70. **a** hamburger
71. **a** bite
72. **a** lolly, **a** chewing gum
73. **an** orange, **an** apple and **a** glass
74. **a** sharpener, **a** biro, **a** green apple
75. **a** fruit gum, **a** lolly, **an** exercise book
76. **an** orange pen , **a** blue rubber, **a** felt pen
77. **a** blue door and **a** green board
78. **an** overhead projector and **a** cassette recorder
79. **a** boy, **a** red car and **an** orange ball
80. **a** black cap, **an** orange, **a** green shirt

pages 4,5

1. **a** cup
2. **an** old house
3. **a** mouse, **an** animal
4. **an** interesting
5. **an** example
6. **a** uniform *pronunciation*: [ju]
7. **a** hat, **an** umbrella
8. **an** ugly colour
9. **an** hour *pron*: [au]
10. **a** European *pron:* [ju]
11. **a** university *pron*: [ju]
12. **a** dentist
13. **an** old book
14. **an** airport
15. **an** accident
16. **a** bad accident
17. **a** very
18. **an** important
19. **an** office
20. **an** American word
21. **an** earring
22. **a** hamburger, **an** orange
23. **an** apple
24. **a** new car, **an** old one
25. **an** orange hat
26. **an** idea, **a** party
27. **a** new umbrella
28. **a** very, **an** apple-pie
29. **a** bottle
30. **an** airport, **an** idea
31. **an** expensive hotel
32. **a** man
33. **an** unhappy girl
34. **an** aunt in France
35. **a** useful *pron*: [ju]
36. **an** island
37. **a** red ear
38. **an** island
39. **an** Austrian schoolboy
40. **an** English schoolboy

41. **an** old locker
42. **an** orange
43. **an** old house
44. **an** expensive bike
45. **an** ordinary cake
46. **an** exam
47. **an** arrogant girl
48. **an** empty glass
49. **a** good story
50. **an** apple, **a** green
51. **a** roll
52. **a** beautiful country
53. **a** new teacher
54. **a** nice teacher
55. **a** funny clown
56. **a** long
57. **an** interesting
58. **an** interesting
59. **a** heavy locker
60. **an** awful noise
61. **a** tasty pizza
62. **an** expensive
63. **a** new camera
64. **an** English breakfast
65. **a** roll, **a** glass and **an** egg
66. **a** superstar
67. **an** orange skateboard
68. **an** awful song
69. **an** overhead projector
70. **a** new English
71. **an** English
72. **an** old castle
73. **an** ice cream
74. **a** beautiful ring
75. **a** bite
76. **a** hamburger and **an** orange juice

pages 7,8

1. is
2. are, am
3. are
4. is, is
5. is
6. is
7. are
8. are
9. is
10. are
11. is
12. are
13. is, is
14. are, am
15. is, is
16. are
17. are
18. is
19. are, are
20. is
21. is
22. are, are
23. are
24. is
25. are
26. is
27. am
28. is, is
29. are, are
30. are
31. are, are
32. is, is
33. are, are
34. are
35. are
36. is
37. is
38. is
39. are
40. are, am
41. is
42. is
43. is
44. are
45. are
46. are
47. are
48. is
49. are, are
50. am
51. are
52. are
53. is
54. are
55. is
56. is
57. are
58. is
59. is
60. are, am
61. are
62. is, is
63. is
64. are
65. is
66. is, are
67. are
68. are
69. is, is
70. are, are
71. is, is
72. is
73. am
74. is
75. are
76. is
77. are, are
78. are, are
79. are
80. are, am
81. are, are

pages 9,10

1. is
2. are
3. is
4. are
5. are
6. are
7. is
8. am
9. are

10. is
11. are
12. are
13. is
14. is
15. is
16. is
17. is
18. is
19. are
20. are
21. are
22. is
23. is
24. is
25. are, am
26. are, am
27. is
28. are
29. are
30. is
31. are
32. is, is
33. are
34. are, am
35. are, am
36. is
37. is
38. is
39. is
40. am
41. are
42. is
43. is
44. is
45. is
46. are
47. is
48. is
49. is
50. are
51. is
52. is
53. are
54. is
55. are, am, am
56. is
57. is, am
58. are, am
59. is
60. is, is
61. is
62. is
63. is
64. are
65. are, are
66. is
67. are, are
68. are, are
69. is, is
70. is, is
71. is, is
72. is
73. is
74. is
75. is
76. is
77. is, is
78. are
79. am, is
80. are
81. is
82. are, is

page 12

Dear Billy,
Thank **you** for **your** letter! How are **you** ? **I** am fine!
I send **you** a photo of **my / our** class. **We** all wear school uniforms.
We look nice in **our** uniforms! **Our** uniforms are super: blue trousers,a blue pullover, a white shirt and **our** ties are red.
Do **you** like the photo?
Have **you** got a brother or a sister? **My** brother is eleven years old.
I have got a sister, too. **Her** name is Sarah. **She** is lovely and **I** like Sarah very much. **We** play very much and **we** have a lot of fun.
Do **you** have a photo of **your** school or **your** house and **your** family?
Have **you** got a pet? **I** have a cat.
Please write back soon!
I am looking forward to **your** letter!

Yours, Peter

This is Sally.
She, her/our, She, Her, her, She, We, she, her.
Look, there`s Bob.
He, He, His, his, He, our/his, We, he.
Look, there are Ben and Bill. **They, They, They, we/they, they/we, We, They/We, Their**

page 13

1. It
2. I , your
3. you, we
4. you, I
5. you, you, I
6. your
7. I / we
8. our / my / their / your, We / They / You
9. I / we/ they/you, I/ We/ They/You, I/ we/ they/you
10. your, your
11. our, We
12. They, They
13. He
14. it, his
15. They
16. She, She
17. They, they
18. She
19. your, it, my
20. We
21. my/ your, I
22. your, It
23. your
24. you, I
25. you, I
26. They
27. her/ my, She

28. I, My
29. your, it, It
30. your,They
31. They
32. They
33. She
34. He
35. they
36. your, It

page 14

1. They, their
2. it
3. you, I
4. Her, She
5. I / We / You They, I / we / you / they
6. your, my
7. it, your
8. They
9. It, He, it
10. their
11. His / Her
12. your
13. their
14. She, her
15. Her
16. my, His, He
17. Their
18. She
19. Our / My, It
20. your, It
21. You
22. They
23. We
24. your, They
25. It, my
26. I, it
27. They
28. It, your
29. you, your, I
30. your, They
31. It
32. he
33. You, I
34. his, It
35. our / my , Its / Our / My
36. It, his
37. it, It

page 15

1. She, her, She
2. I, We, Our
3. their, They
4. He, his
5. I, We, our
6. It, her, She, her
7. I, We, We, our
8. their, They
9. you, your
10. I, We, our, We
11. his
12. my, I
13. They
14. your / my , my / your
15. their
16. your, It
17. I, We, We
18. its
19. Our / My , She
20. you, I, I, my
21. He, his
22. your, it, my, My
23. They, I / We, they
24. She, her
25. We/ They, We / They
26. your / his , it, My / His
27. They, it
28. my / his / her / our, Her, she
29. I / We / You / They, It / She / He , its / her / his

> *Achtung: Wenn das Geschlecht des Haustieres bekannt ist, verwendet man he / she bzw. his / her*

30. I / We, my / our, She, her

page 16

1. his, He, He, His
2. my / our, She / He, her / his
3. I / We / You / They , They
4. you, I
5. Its, its, It
6. His
7. my
8. I / you, I, I, my
9. I / We / You / They, They
10. you, I, it
11. your, it, my
12. My / Our, I / We, her
13. her, she
14. my / our, Its
15. my, you, it
16. He, his
17. She, it
18. Our / My / Your / Their , He
19. Its
20. They
21. their, They
22. you, I, my
23. Her
24. you, I
25. His, It
26. Our / Their
27. His
28. his
29. his / her
30. your, my
31. my
32. your, my, My
33. My / Your / Our

page 17

Simon says: your 7x, his 5x, her 7x, their 7x

1. Her
2. Our
3. his
4. His
5. Their
6. Her
7. her
8. His
9. His
10. their

page 19

1. have
2. have
3. have
4. has
5. have
6. have
7. has
8. has
9. have
10. have
11. has
12. has
13. has
14. has
15. have
16. Have
17. has
18. have
19. has
20. has
21. have
22. Have, have
23. have
24. has
25. have
26. have
27. has
28. has
29. has
30. have
31. have
32. have
33. have
34. has
35. has

page 21

1. hides
2. are am
3. are are
4. takes
5. sit, play
6. washes, goes
7. have
8. is
9. misses
10. have, is
11. wipes
12. meet
13. can
14. gives
15. like, likes
16. says
17. sing
18. buy
19. comes
20. are
21. must
22. say
23. tries
24. try
25. listen
26. is
27. needs
28. makes
29. thank
30. take, open
31. go, buy
32. pays
33. listen
34. has, has
35. can, can

page 22

1. are
2. takes
3. go
4. want
5. orders
6. colours
7. looks
8. meet
9. has, goes
10. can
11. must
12. jumps, turns
13. wears, likes
14. has
15. points
16. can
17. hides
18. drinks
19. wants
20. must, is
21. has
22. say, are
23. cries, is
24. wears
25. goes, go
26. look
27. looks
28. wants
29. go
30. has
31. need
32. forgets
33. asks, goes
34. loves
35. think, looks
36. wants, needs
37. cleans
38. writes
39. play

page 23

1. gives, likes
2. thinks, are
3. are
4. shuts, goes
5. listens
6. hates, has
7. have
8. eat
9. goes
10. has
11. are
12. dances
13. hates
14. hands
15. knows
16. can
17. likes, hates
18. runs, is
19. have
20. come
21. eat, drink
22. plays
23. pays
24. am, must, is
25. has, wants
26. makes, bakes
27. has
28. does
29. writes
30. make
31. tries, are

page 26

1. Can he come ?
2. Is the party... ?
3. Is Sally happy ?
4. Do the children meet Nora ?
5. Must Sandy do her homework ?
6. Is the caterpillar in the grass ?
7. Is the mouse under ...?
8. Has Peter got a rabbit ?
9. Are the children in ...?
10. Is the monkey on the elephant ?
11. Does the pullover suit her?
12. Does Sandra wipe the chocolate ..... ?
13. Do all children come to ...?
14. Does Mick open .....?
15. Does father like classical music ?
16. Do we all wear uniforms ...?
17. Do you like grey?
18. Does Peter go to school by bus?
19. Do we go to .... ?
20. Does Mary buy flowers ......?
21. Does Max order....?
22. Does Sally jump for joy ?
23. Does the baby put its toes into its mouth?
24. Are we / you penfriends?
25. Are my / your new trousers red?
26. Does she wipe the ice cream off her jacket?
27. Does Peter hold Mary`s hand?
28. Can she come in?
29. Has Fred got a snake at home?
30. Is the window open?
31. Is the blouse expensive?
32. Are uniforms boring?
33. Is Frank a very nice boy?
34. Must we leave now?
35. Are her shoes 50 pounds?
36. Is her garden full of flowers?
37. Has Willie got a photo of ...?
38. Does mother like butterflies?
39. Does Molly stand up?

page 27

1. Does Fred hate lollies?
2. Does Billy turn around?
3. Does Mick Jagger write a new song?
4. Does he put his hand on the table?
5. Does mother iron my dress?
6. Does the teacher hand out ....?
7. Does Ann meet Mary in front ...?
8. Does the pizzaman take the pizza to ....?
9. Do we often buy ice cream?
10. Is her skirt expensive?
11. Must we be quiet in class?
12. Must Peter help in the kitchen?
13. Are you clever?
14. Does the parrot eat ... ?
15. Does the monkey eat bananas?
16. Do the monkeys eat bananas?
17. Is the pen in the cupboard?
18. Is my new coat in the locker?
19. Has Peter got a new bike?
20. Must Sally help in ...?
21. Do the children play ....?
22. Can we / you spell ... ?
23. Do elephants eat grass?
24. Do all children like ice cream?
25. Has Sally got a nice friend?
26. Does Paul hate spiders ?
27. Are they Austrian?
28. Can monkeys climb trees?
29. Is Phil`s book boring?
30. Have we got ...?
31. Does mother take Susan to ....?
32. Do the children often watch TV?
33. Does Pit listen to ...?
34. Does Mary play with ...?
35. Does father take Ben to ....?
36. Does Laura like popcorn?
37. Do the Millers go to Italy?
38. Can Nancy play the recorder ?

page 28

I) Have or has

1. have, has
2. have
3. have
4. have
5. has
6. have, has
7. have
8. have

II) Fill in the correct form of the verb:

1. don't, is

2. Is, isn't
3. suits, like
4. take out, are
5. goes
6. touches
7. takes
8. says
9. jumps, turns
10. listen
11. does
12. are, is
13. am not, am

III) a / an
1. an
2. an, a
3. an
4. a
5. a

page 29

IV) Ask questions:
1. Does Peter go ...?
2. Do we / you meet ...?
3. Does the teacher hand out ...?
4. Does the monkey take the banana?
5. Is Tom hungry?
6. Has Tony got a brother?
7. Are they at Sarah's party?
8. Do you like bananas ?
9. Does he go to school?
10. Does she want a lolly?
11. Are we / you ready ?
12. Does Tony like sweets?
13. Is the cat on the chair?
14. Does Pam want another dress ?
15. Does mother iron my shirt?
16. Do they listen to ...?
17. Do I / you like uniforms ?
18. Do we / you run to school?

V) They`re , there, their:
1. There
2. their
3. They're, They're
4. Their
5. There
6. They're
7. There
8. There
9. They're
10. There
11. their, They're
12. There
13. their, They're
14. There
15. there, their
16. there. They're

page 30

1. Its
2. It's
3. It's
4. It's
5. its
6. It's
7. Its
8. It's
9. It's
10. It's
11. It's, its
12. It's, its
13. It's, Its
14. It's
15. Its
16. It's
17. It's
18. It's
19. It's
20. It's, It's
21. It's
22. it's
23. Its
24. Its
25. It's
26. It's
27. It's
28. It's
29. its, it's, its
30. It's
31. its, it's
32. It's
33. It's
34. It's
35. its
36. It's
37. It's
38. its

page 31

1. What is (What's) your name?
2. What is (What's) your telephone number?
3. What colour is your schoolbag (satchel)?
4. Do you want (like) a chewing gum?
5. What flavour is your ice cream?
6. Are you ready?
7. Do you like (want) cornflakes?
8. What colour **are** your trousers?
9. Do you like (want) yoghurt?
10. How much is the shirt?
11. What flavour is the lolly?
12. Are you thirsty?
13. Are you hungry?
14. Have you got (Do you have) a cold?
15. Do you come to my party?
16. Can I have your rubber?
17. Do you like (want) oranges?
18. Have you got (Do you have) a sister?
19. Have you got toothache?
20. Are you tired?
21. How much **are** the tights?
22. Where is my pen?
23. What is 'P.' in English?

24. How much is the cap?
25. What do monkeys eat?
26. When do you come back?
27. When do you do your homework?
28. Where is my new blouse?
29. How are you today?
30. What's the name of your new English teacher?
31. What's the time, please?
32. What's for breakfast? (What do we have for b.?)
33. Have you got stomachache?
34. Have you got **a** headache?
35. Does your knee hurt?
36. Can you touch your toes?
37. Is the wastepaper basket full?
38. Can you help me?
39. Have you got (Do you have) a penfriend?

page 33

1. His trousers **are** great.
2. Her tights **are** old.
3. Her trousers **are** yellow.
4. His jeans **are** old.
5. Mary`s pants **are** pink.
6. Paint a butterfly on your trousers!
7. Iron your trousers!
8. Put on your trousers! (Put your t.on.)
9. The trousers **are** eighty pounds.
10. How much **are** the trousers? They are ninety pounds.
11. Do you want the coat medium or large?
12. **I'll** take it x-large.
13. How much are the trainers? They are fifty-five pounds.
14. How much is the T-shirt with the flower on it?
15. It is only twenty pounds. That's cheap.I'll take it.
16. Bake a cake!
17. Do your homework!
18. Her trousers **are** super!
19. His pants **are** new.
20. My tights **are** OK.
21. I cannot (can't) come to your party.
22. Let's play catch!
23. I have (got) terrible earache.
24. I have (got) **a** caugh and **a** headache.
25. I'm not so fine today. (I'm not very well today.)
26. How are you today?
27. How do you feel today?
28. Don't buy the dog. It is too big.
29. Let me go home!
30. Let me see!
31. Leave me alone!
32. Don't keep me waiting!
33. Don't chat with your neighbour!
34. Let us go!(Let's go!)
35. Help her!
36. I have got **a** sore throat.
37. Let's play 'Catch the thief'!
38. It's five past five.
39. It's quarter to eight.

pages 35/36/37

1. I haven't got......
2. He isn't a nice boy.
3. We don't go to a party.
4. She doesn't write a letter.
5. We aren't happy.
6. They aren't sad.
7. He doesn't sing a song.
8. He hasn't got a pencil.
9. I don't go to his party.
10. Cathy isn't hungry.
11. Peter isn't in the garden.
12. We don't say "Hello".
13. You don't run to Peter.
14. She doesn't go to town.
15. We aren't hungry.
16. She hasn't got a sister.
17. We haven't got a new pullover.
18. They don't eat a cake.
19. Ann doesn't bend her knees.
20. Mother doesn't iron my shirt.
21. They don't listen to the teacher.
22. Pam doesn't want new trousers.
23. They don't listen to the music.
24. Tony doesn't like ice cream.
25. The monkey doesn't take the banana to ....
26. We don't eat a cake.
27. They don't touch the floor.
28. It isn't nice.
29. This isn't a photo of our school.
30. I don't like uniforms.
31. Bob isn't clever.
32. I haven't got a pet.
33. His hair isn't black.
34. Tom hasn't got a pet.
35. We don't iron our shirts.
36. My sister doesn't iron my blouse.
37. Children don't love sweets.
38. Sandy doesn't stand up.
39. Billy doesn't jump high.
40. The cat isn't on the chair.
41. You aren't in the garden.
42. We aren't at home.
43. We don't eat a sandwich.
44. She doesn't want a lolly.
45. My brother doesn't go to school.
46. You don't like bananas.
47. Don't come to Bob!
48. Don't go to the circus!
49. Peter doesn't go to the party.
50. You don't run fast.
51. Sally doesn't write a poem.
52. Tony hasn't got a brother.
53. We don't meet our friends.
54. The cat isn't hungry.
55. We aren't sleepy.
56. He doesn't like jeans.
57. He isn't a funny teacher.
58. Sarah isn't nice.
59. We don't wear uniforms.
60. I don't like wearing skirts.
61. He isn't new at our school.
62. I don't think he is nice.(I think he isn't...)
63. He doesn't look at the photo.
64. He isn't cool.
65. His eyes aren't blue.
66. His name isn't Smith.

67. I don't like our school.
68. She doesn't like wearing trousers.
69. We don't turn around.
70. She doesn't open the window.
71. Tim isn't quiet.
72. Liz doesn't shut the book.
73. The frog isn't behind the curtain.
74. He doesn't take the book to Peter.
75. I don't love toffees.
76. The monkey doesn't eat popcorn.
77. They don't catch the thief.
78. Elephants don't eat grass.
79. Snakes don't love eggs.
80. He doesn't stamp his feet.
81. I haven't got toothache.
82. My knee doesn't hurt.
83. Don't be quiet !
84. Don't write a song !
85. Don't shut the window !
86. Don't stand up !
87. Don't turn around !
88. Don't shake your hair !
89. Don't play hide and seek!
90. Don't go to the blackboard !
91. Peter doesn't like hamburgers.
92. Ann isn't at home.
93. He doesn't like wearing dark colours.
94. Don't sit down !
95. Mandy hasn't got a sister.
96. She isn't lovely.
97. We don't go to a restaurant.
98. He doesn't run to school.
99. She doesn't like apples very much.
100. I don't like coffee.
101. Pam doesn't open the door.
102. Pit isn't ill.
103. Father doesn't work in the garden.
104. The children don't play hide and seek.
105. It isn't a wonderful day.
106. I don't buy a toothbrush.
107. Frank doesn't eat strawberries.
108. Pamela doesn't like popcorn.
109. We don't go to the circus.
110. The frog doesn't jump into the pond.
111. Mother doesn't make a plan for the week.
112. We don't write a list.
113. The children don't go to the playground.
114. The girls don't play with their dolls.
115. I haven't got a brother and a sister.
116. He cannot (can't) jump around.
117. Peter cannot (can't) open the box.

page 40

stories
toes
boxes
lollies
monkeys
stars
dresses
apples
toothbrushes
women
men
books
mice
toffees
oranges
desks
sandwiches
fruit gums
cameras
boys
strawberries
parties
classes
boxes
inches
children
feet
teeth
geese
knives
wolves
calves
crocodiles
ladies
cities
lives
watches
kisses
buses
flies
bushes
glasses
foxes
oxen
horses
fish
matches
keys
wives
toys
days
tomatoes
potatoes
Eskimos
cliffs
leaves
roofs
thieves
berries
babies
lice
pens
fish
sheep
deer
handkerchiefs
photos
satchels
houses
glasses
cows
brushes
teachers
cars

page 41

dogs
doors
painters
bikes
computers
shelves
pencils
pupils
sharpeners
notes
recorders
dialogues
brothers
bananas
cups
caps
trees
dreams

TRANSLATE:

1) Fish swim in the river.
2) Our sheep eat grass.
3) My trousers are great !
4) His teeth hurt.
5) Mice like cheese.
6) The foxes catch the geese.
7) Foxes hide in bushes.
8) Wolves are dangerous.
9) All leaves fall off the tree.
10) Many dogs have got lice.
11) The glasses are full.
12) Where are Tim's trousers?
13) My feet hurt.
14) The stories are interesting.
15) The shelves are long.
16) We catch the thieves.
17) Do you like strawberries?
18) The babies cry.
19) Mice are small.
20) Let's hide behind the bushes.
21) My glasses are new.
22) My tights are black.
23) Flies are ugly.
24) How many sandwiches does he eat?
25) Lollies are sweet.
26) I like tomatoes.
27) I buy two loaves of bread.

page 43

1. Yes, I am. No, I'm not.
2. Yes, he is. No, he isn't.
3. Yes, it is. No, it isn't.
4. Yes, we are. No, we aren't.
5. Yes, they are. No, they aren't.
6. Yes, I can. No, I cannot. No, I can't.
7. Yes, I have. No, I haven't.
8. Yes, they can. No, they can't.
9. Yes, she has. No, she hasn't.
10. Yes, they are. No, they aren't.
11. Yes, they have. No, they haven't.
12. Yes, you can. No, you can't.
13. Yes, I do. No, I don't.
14. Yes, it is. No, it isn't.
15. Yes, I have. No, I haven't.
16. Yes, I can. No, I can't.
17. Yes, there is. No, there isn't.
18. Yes, he is. No, he isn't.
19. Yes, I do. No, I don't.
20. Yes, I am. No, I am not. I'm not.
21. Yes, there is. No, there isn't.
22. Yes, he can. No, he can't.
23. Yes, I have. No, I haven't.
24. Yes, I can. No, I can't.
25. Yes, I do. No, I don't.
26. Yes, he does. No, he doesn't.
27. Yes, he has. No, he hasn't.
28. Yes, I can. No, I can't.
29. Yes, I do. No, I don't.
30. Yes, he is. No, he isn't.
31. Yes, I am. No, I'm not.
32. Yes, he is. No, he isn' t.
33. Yes, I do. No, I don't.
34. Yes, he does. No, he doesn't.
35. Yes, he does. No, he doesn't.
36. Yes, I can. No, I can't.

page 45

1. They, them.
2. it
3. them
4. it, them
5. them
6. them
7. him / her
8. them
9. them
10. it
11. them
12. them
13. them
14. them
15. them
16. He,it
17. it
18. She, it
19. They, it
20. She, it
21. it, him
22. We, them
23. them
24. them, him
25. him
26. them, them
27. it, her
28. They, them
29. her, It
30. him, their
31. You
32. We
33. They, them
34. us
35. her
36. his
37. their

page 46

38. them
39. them
40. their
41. her
42. my
43. me/us, your
44. it, his
45. her
46. They
47. us
48. us
49. it
50. it
51. me
52. him
53. you
54. I, them
55. them
56. She
57. them
58. me
59. us, it
60. you
61. her
62. him
63. you, them
64. them
65. She, her, her
66. her
67. him
68. it
69. them
70. them
71. his
72. them
73. it
74. them
75. it
76. it
77. his, him

page 47

1. her
2. us
3. He, his / She, her
4. their
5. her
6. I, you
7. They
8. She
9. our
10. him
11. your, it, I
12. They
13. her, it
14. you
15. them
16. its
17. him
18. its
19. your
20. my
21. them
22. you
23. me / us
24. our, our
25. you, us
26. them, their
27. her
28. her
29. us
30. it , his, He
31. me, it
32. it, its
33. their, them
34. them

page 48

35. her
36. it
37. him
38. you, them
39. I, him
40. me
41. I, it
42. It, him
43. I, you
44. I, them, it
45. you
46. them
47. it, him
48. they, their
49. her
50. he, his, He, his, him
51. her
52. us
53. It, wenn Geschlecht bekannt: He / She
54. you, I, you
55. Her, she
56. They, him
57. We / They / You / I
58. We
59. He, they
60. me, you
61. you, I
62. She, her
63. He
64. We
65. they
66. It
67. It
68. It, She
69. you, them
70. them

page 49

1. them
2. She, them
3. He
4. They, them
5. She
6. It, her
7. They
8. it
9. He
10. It / She / He
11. it

12. it, him
13. her
14. his
15. him
16. them
17. He
18. They
19. We
20. him
21. them
22. They
23. it, him
24. It
25. They
26. They, him / her
27. We, him
28. us
29. her
30. You, them
31. them
32. it, them
33. our
34. He, them
35. She, them
36. They, it, her
37. it, him

page 53

1. is T. doing, is writing
2. is
3. is juggling
4. speaks
5. watch, am watching
6. open, close
7. starts, comes
8. goes
9. is singing
10. have
11. feel
12. plays
13. goes, is having
14. is sleeping
15. moves
16. is, speaks
17. gets up, has, goes
18. are you doing, am listening
19. goes
20. does not eat, has
21. is not, rains
22. smokes
23. go
24. doesn't eat
25. is playing
26. are having
27. is swimming

page 54

28. am coming
29. Is it snowing, is raining
30. are standing
31. is coming
32. stay
33. speaks
34. do you usually spend, fly
35. are you doing, am looking
36. washes
37. wash
38. does, is staying, has/is having
39. does he drink
40. plays, isn't playing
41. am working, must work
42. reads, is listening
43. have, are only drinking
44. plays, is playing
45. is listening
46. cleans
47. is waiting
48. play
49. am doing
50. is writing
51. is telling
52. like
53. is climbing

page 55

1. is having
2. is raining
3. am not listening
4. are you doing
5. drinks
6. reads
7. finishes, is still writing
8. is sitting, is reading
9. are playing
10. are having, phone
11. are not listening
12. is ringing
13. am not watching
14. am staying
15. am having
16. speak, is having, phone
17. goes
18. finishes, is still working
19. is still raining, can't / cannot go
20. go, am still reading
21. goes, is walking
22. drives
23. is singing
24. reads, is cleaning
25. is

page 56

26. feels
27. Do you often eat
28. arrives
29. has, is eating
30. have
31. is not doing, is phoning
32. fall
33. goes
34. do you usually do, read, watch, play
35. feels
36. watches
37. find
38. meets
39. bakes

40. are sitting
41. opens
42. is doing
43. does
44. goes, is having
45. are running
46. walks, says
47. am doing
48. are having
49. watches
50. are playing, come
51. do
52. help, am feeding
53. are you eating, am eating
54. shut

page 57

1. ask, I am listening
2. is writing
3. walks, goes
4. are riding
5. help, am testing
6. are you eating, am eating
7. watches
8. get, have
9. goes
10. get
11. watch
12. go
13. do
14. goes, is watching
15. wash
16. goes, stays
17. barks
18. catches
19. gets
20. likes
21. is smoking
22. is singing / are singing
23. is working
24. are doing
25. is snowing
26. collects
27. are running

page 58

28. visits
29. is starting
30. brings
31. speak, is sleeping
32. is crying, cry
33. look at
34. are you looking, know
35. think
36. eat
37. come, am playing
38. drink
39. come, am looking, find
40. goes, is staying up
41. do you see, is wearing
42. goes, goes
43. come, am baking, stay
44. am coming
45. writes, is writing
46. do
47. are listening
48. am watching
49. is running
50. go
51. washes
52. ask

page 61

1. Who often runs, When do we often run....
2. Who eats, Whose sandwich does Sandy eat ?
3. Who buys, What does father buy, When does father buy...
4. Who can sing, What can the girl do, What can the girl sing ?
5. Who is watching, What are we doing....
6. What is Bill not good at?
7. Who always has, What do they always have ...
8. Who always listens to, When does mother always listen to the news ?
9. Who has got, What have we got, How many times have we got...
10. What has Sandy got?
11. Who is just working, Where are we just working?
12. Whose sister does he like?
13. What does Pat want to have?
14. What is Maggie paying for?
15. Why must you / I help me / you .....
16. What can you / I have?
17. Where do the children play ..., When do the children play near the river ?
18. Who must we look for?
19. What does Sandy look for?
20. Who cannot eat everyth., What can he not do?
21. What does Bob like to do?
22. Where is the aeroplane flying?
23. What does Tom like to do?
24. Who goes to a birthday party at Mary's house?
25. What colour is his satchel?
26. Who helps .....,Who does the girl help..., Where does the girl help her mother?
27. What is holding...,Where is the c.holding a ...
28. What has Milly got?
29. Why does Peter go ...?
30. What does the boy want?
31. What kind of cake does Trish love?
32. When do we do...?
33. What do they listen to?
34. What has she got?
35. What does the dog do?
36. Who do we visit..., When do we visit...
37. Who brushes his ....., When do they brush their...?
38. Who is there a letter for?
39. When do we wait for the bus?

page 62

40. Whose little sister do I / you love?
41. When does the plane leave?
42. Who is she waiting for?

43. What does he get from his...., Who does he get a present from ..?
44. Whose cassette does Ann listen to?, Where does Ann listen to Bill's cassette ?
45. What colour is our school uniform?
46. How much are the trousers?
47. What does mother sew for Mary?, Who does mother sew a new dress for?
48. When do I / you always go to town?
49. Whose books does Peter like?
50. Who buys food, When do the ch.buy food?
51. What can Tom sing?
52. What is Tony listening to?
53. What is Bob good at?
54. Who always has ..., What do we always have for breakfast?
55. When does father always listen to the news?
56. When are we always at school?
57. What has Tony got?
58. What does Tony have?
59. Who is just doing..., What are we just doing?
60. Whose book do you like?
61. Who wants to have...,What do you want to have?
62. When does she buy some apples?
63. What is he just reading?
64. When does Ann always go to school?
65. When does he never watch TV?
66. Who is paying...,What are the ch. paying for?
67. What must you dry?
68. What can she have?
69. Who plays ....., Where do the children play every day?
70. What must we do?
71. What is she looking for?
72. What can he not / can't he do?
73. When does Tony always go to school?
74. Who do we visit in..., When do we visit Uncle Marc?
75. What does she wash every day? When does she wash her hair?
76. How much is the dress?
77. When does the train leave?
78. What must Sally look for?
79. Why does Joe go to bed?

page 63

1. Who is running up the hill?
2. What is flying..., Where is the bird flying?
3. What does the dog like to do? Where does the dog like to jump (into)?
4. Who goes to a party.....?
5. Where is Sally sitting?
6. Whose birthday is it?
7. Whose nose is red? What colour is....?
8. Who goes ...., Where do the boys go(to)?
9. What does Pam throw into..., Where does Pam throw a stone?
10. What is the dog holding.....,Where is the dog holding a stick?
11. What has Maggie got?
12. Who wants some sweets ?,What do the children want?
13. Who is good at playing tennis? What am I/are you good at?
14. What does Trish like?
15. What is Billy doing?,When is B.writing a l.?
16. Who is a clever boy?
17. Who buys some oranges?, What do we buy?
18. What can I / you do alone?
19. When does she eat her lunch?
20. What does mother shut?
21. What does father buy?
22. Who brushes his teeth....?, When do we brush our teeth?
23. What leaves at nine pm.?,When does the train leave?
24. Where does Pat read his book?
25. Who is there a parcel for?
26. What does she draw?
27. Who do I / you get a letter from twice a month?, How often do I / you get...
28. Why does Sandy eat a sandwich?
29. Who must clean his / our room?
30. Who must we listen to?
31. What does he look at?
32. What does she sew on her jeans?
33. What does he take to his friend?, Where does he take the present to? Who does he take ...
34. What does he help me with?
35. Why does Trish go to bed?
36. What colour is my / your new coat?
37. What is one p.?,How much are the apples?
38. What does she like?
39. What does mother buy for Tom? Who does mother buy a new pullover for?

page 64

40. Who does he call in the evening?, When does he call me?
41. Whose bike don't we find / do we not find?
42. What may we see?
43. What must Sandy look for?
44. How many pizzas can he eat?
45. What does she want?
46. What does he show to the teacher? Who does he show his work to?
47. How many stamps does Mr Miller buy for his letters? What does Mr M.buy six stamps for?
48. What can the children do?
49. What has Sally got?
50. How does her grey sweater look?
51. When does she wear her jeans skirt?
52. Whose tights are too long?
53. What does Peter drink in the morning?
54. What does he get from his aunt?, Who does he get a present from?
55. Why does Sally go to bed?
56. When does mother always go to market?
57. Who is sleeping?
58. What does Pat usually have for breakfast?
59. What can R.not find? / What can't R.find?
60. Why does Pit run to school?
61. Where is the new coat from?
62. Who does Mary stay with?
63. Whose new hat is this?
64. Why is Tom sad?
65. What must Pam look for?
66. What do the children eat?
67. Who is swimming in the pond?, Where are Sue and Tom swimming?

68. What kind of ice cream do we prefer? / What flavour do we prefer?
69. What is there in front of his house?, Where is there a nut tree?
70. Whose model car is this?
71. What does father wash every week?
72. How many pizzas does Charles eat?
73. How does Fred always go to school?
74. Who does Aunt Mary stay with?
75. Who do we like?
76. What kind of cake does Pam like?
77. Whose newspaper is this?
78. Who have we got a nice present for?
79. What is she doing in the garden?
80. What make is his car?

page 66

1. some
2. an
3. some
4. a
5. some
6. some
7. some
8. some
9. some
10. an
11. a, some
12. some
13. some
14. some
15. a, a
16. some
17. a
18. some
19. a
20. some
21. an
22. some
23. some
24. some, some
25. a, some
26. a
27. some
28. a
29. some, some
30. a
31. some / an
32. some
33. some, some

page 67

34. some
35. a /some
36. some
37. some
38. some
39. a, some
40. some
41. an, a, some
42. some, some
43. some
44. some, some
45. an, a, a, some
46. some
47. some
48. some
49. some
50. some
51. some
52. a
53. some / a, a
54. some
55. some, some
56. some
57. a, some
58. a
59. some
60. some
61. some
62. some
63. some
64. a
65. some, some
66. a
67. some
68. some
69. some
70. some
71. some

page 69

1. brothers'
2. sister's
3. parents'
4. James's
5. Paul's
6. hour's
7. sisters'
8. hour's, hours'
9. baker's
10. minute's
11. dentist's
12. Tim's
13. children**'s**
14. dog's
15. sister's
16. women**'s**
17. stone's
18. parents'
19. Smiths'
20. Donald's
21. yesterday's
22. today's
23. Frank's
24. Mr Lampton's
25. Sarah's
26. Mandy's
27. hour's
28. brothers'
29. Keith's
30. Joe's
31. weeks'
32. Tom's
33. The Carters'
34. sister's
35. children's
36. hours'

37. evening's
38. week's

page 71

1. this
2. this, that
3. this
4. that
5. This
6. that
7. this, that
8. this
9. this
10. this, that
11. These, those
12. this
13. this
14. that
15. That
16. this
17. that
18. These
19. these
20. those
21. this
22. This, that
23. These, those
24. those
25. these
26. those
27. This
28. this
29. these, those
30. this, that
31. these
32. those , That
33. These, those
34. these
35. These, those

page 72

36. This
37. those
38. this
39. that
40. that
41. this, that
42. This
43. that
44. this
45. this
46. this
47. this, that
48. This
49. these
50. This, that
51. this
52. this
53. these
54. These
55. This, that
56. this
57. These, those
58. this
59. This
60. that
61. That
62. these, those
63. those
64. that
65. These
66. this
67. this
68. that
69. this
70. that

page 74

1. Jill reads a newspaper every day.
2. I don't like football very much.
3. I always forget my watch in the bathroom in the morning.
4. We do the same thing every day.
5. I don't like this picture very much.
6. Mother puts her money in her handbag in the morning.
7. Every day she smokes two cigarettes before breakfast / She smokes two cigarettes before breakfast every day.
8. We meet some friends at the c. this evening.
9. He does not wear the same clothes every day.
10. George walks to work every morning.
11. We arrive at the party early in the evening.
12. I usually go to bed early in the evening.
13. Tom goes to Italy in summer every year./ Every year Tom goes to Italy in summer.
14. I have my breakfast in bed in the morning.
15. Barbara will go to University in October. / In October Barbara will go to University.
16. I always forget my umbr. in the bus in the m..
17. She watches TV all evening.
18. We invite a lot of p.to the party today evening
19. It was a great birthday party yesterday.
20. My neighbour never speaks to me.
21. Susan is always polite.
22. I finish work at half past ten every night.
23. She rarely goes to bed before m..
24. He doesn't often eat meat.
25. I can never rem.his name.
26. The bus is usually not late.
27. He is still in bed.
28. He is never ill.
29. It is often very cold here in winter.
30. What do you usually have for breakfast?
31. She is always tired in the evening.
32. Do you often eat in restaurants?
33. I sometimes eat too much.
34. He always goes to work by car in the morning / In the morn. he always goes to work by car.
35. Pit often plays tennis in the afternoon./ In the afternoon Pit often plays tennis.
36. She sometimes feels sad.
37. Bob is never sad .
38. They usually have dinner at seven o`clock in the evening.

page 75

39. They all live in London.
40. Pit also plays footb. and bb.two times a week.
41. Both my brothers are doctors.
42. I will always remember you.
43. Do you usually go home by bus after school?
44. I can never find my keys when I come home.
45. In summer it rarely snows.
46. He must always do his homework in the afternoon.
47. She will arrive at 7 o'clock tomorrow evening./Tomorow ev. she will arrive at 7...
48. Ann goes to school every day. /Every day Ann goes to school.
49. They often eat bananas in the morning.
50. Sandy never has a headache.
51. The children often buy a hamb. at McD's.
52. Ann often wears jeans to school.
53. A. cannot eat all the nice things..
54. Cindy is not at home but she is at school.
55. Peter is just having his breakfast.
56. Do you like apples?
57. Your brother is listening to music..
58. When do you usually have b. in the morning?
59. The cat is standing in front of the mousehole but it doesn't see a mouse.
60. What time do you go to school every day?
61. Tony often meets his friends in the p. at 4pm..
62. What are you good at ?
63. I am good at skiing but I don't like skating.
64. Mandy often writes a postcard to her penfriend in England.
65. The children like to speak English at school.
66. Pat's room is full of posters of animals.
67. My mother loves romantic films but I hate them.
68. Every day the boys play in the playground./ The boys play in the playground every day.
69. The children must pay for the hamburger.
70. Tony has got a new watch for his birthday.
71. I want to have the green pencil, please.
72. On Monday we eat at twelve o'clock./ We eat at 12 o'cl. on Monday.
73. They are usually at home in the evening./ In the evening they are usually at home.
74. Bob is never ill in winter.
75. We rarely watch TV in the afternoon.
76. Bob takes the present to his friend.
77. He shows his homework to the teacher in the morning. / In the morning he shows his homework to the teacher.

page 79

1. was, is
2. is, was
3. am
4. was, gave
5. were
6. are
7. were
8. is
9. was
10. were, arrived
11. went
12. was
13. are,were
14. did not like, was, wasn't
15. phoned, weren't
16. wasn't, was, is
17. were
18. Were you, wasn't, was
19. saw
20. Did you watch, watch
21. went, was, liked
22. is, was
23. was
24. was, was
25. were you
26. are, did you buy
27. was he
28. had

page 80

1. Who was a. ...
2. Who went to .., Where did Bob go (to)? / Who did Bob go to ?
3. What did Simon ask Sally for?
4. When did our grandparents come?
5. What did the monkey hide in the tree?
6. What did Peter look for?
7. What could they not find?
8. What kind of film did Bob watch?
9. What did mother pour into my glass? Where did mother pour milk?
10. What did she sew?
11. Where did they sit?
12. What parked near our house?
13. Why did they have to run to school?
14. What did Sandy eat?
15. What was Bill not good at?
16. What did Pam want to have?
17. What could she not do / couldn't she do alone?
18. Who did we have to look for?
19. What did Tom want to climb?
20. Where did the children go (to)?.
21. Where did Maggie help her mother?
22. What colour was his schoolbag?
23. Where did Mr Simons live?
24. Why did Peter go to bed?
25. What did the dog run after?
26. Who did we visit in our holidays? When did we visit Aunt Mary?
27. When did we do a lot of work?
28. When / What time in the morning did the plane leave?
29. Who did she wait for?
30. What did he get from Uncle Marc? Who did he get a toy car from?
31. What colour were their uniforms?
32. Where did Ann listen to cassettes?
33. How much was the dress?
34. Who did Mum sew a dark blue dress for?
35. How many pizzas did Charles eat?
36. What did he get in English?
37. What did they look at?
38. Who did we / you like very much?

page 81

39. How many slices of cake did Sandy eat?
40. Whose old cap was this?
41. Where did he always go by bus?, How did he always go to work?
42. Who did we meet in the park? Where did we meet Robert?
43. When did he do his homework?
44. How often did he clean his shoes ?
45. Who went to ...? When did they go to church?
46. Where did they live?
47. Who came in the evening?
48. Where did he come from?.
49. When did he go skiing?
50. What did Susan write to her penfriend? Who did Susan write a letter to?
51. What did father bring for Tom? Who did father bring a present for?
52. Who bought warm tights for Susan? Who did Mum buy warm tights for?
53. When did Pit ride his bike?
54. What did we / you have to clean?
55. Where did they make a trip to?
56. What did I get from my friend in Paris? Who did I get a letter from?
57. What did we / you buy at the market? Where did we / you buy some oranges?
58. What did we / you look at?
59. What did he take to his friend? Who did he take the present to?
60. When did Pit read his book?
61. Where did Paul call me from in the evening?
62. Whose birthday was it?
63. Why did mother shut the window?
64. What colour was my / your old coat?
65. What did mother make?
66. What did we / you cook?
67. Who did she say 'Hello' to?
68. What did Pat tell us? Who did Pat tell the truth to?(3.Fall!)
69. Who went by taxi? How did we / you go?
70. What hit their car? What did a big stone hit?
71. Where did the children hide?
72. What did Mary sing?
73. Where did Dad take us (to) ?
74. Who shook hands? What did they do?
75. When did the bell ring? / What time did ....?

page 83

1. Were you, wasn't, had, had to
2. are going to go
3. spent, had, went, ate, played, were
4. did not see / didn't see
5. goes / went , think, is / was
6. is crying
7. was, broke
8. are you going to do, am going to ride
9. Did you listen to, didn't have, had to
10. drinks, is drinking
11. are, were, are hiding
12. called, was
13. is going to be
14. could not / couldn't, was
15. am going to have
16. were, are
17. watch, must go / have to go

page 84

18. are you doing, am writing, Do you need
19. is going to come
20. is, like
21. is putting
22. sleeps, cannot / can't, is crying
23. Do you like, are
24. are you doing / are you going to do, I am cutting / am going to cut
25. ate up
26. went
27. bought, wasn't / was not
28. watch
29. is going to buy
30. has, was
31. is going to write
32. set, sets
33. brought, has
34. Did you hear, didn't hear
35. goes, went, was
36. slept, didn't hear
37. met, was
38. are you going to build, are still looking for
39. is snowing

page 85

1. When were the children very tired? Who was very tired last night?
2. What did Sandy eat?
3. When is he going to come?
4. What is Mary singing?
5. Why didn' t Fred go to school? Why did Fred not go to school?
6. Where do they go (to) on Sundays? When do they go to a restaurant?
7. What did they have for dinner?
8. When does grandfather sleep?
9. Where are Liz and her sister going to spend their holidays?
10. What does he like for breakfast?
11. When did they often go to the cinema?
12. What are they cutting out?
13. Who did Uncle Marc visit last Saturday?
14. Who sometimes goes skiing in winter?, When do we sometimes go skiing?
15. What are they drinking now?
16. What is Pam going to bake for the weekend?
17. When does the concert begin?
18. Where are the Fishers going to make a trip (to)?
19. What have they got there?
20. What are the children playing?
21. How did we / you travel last summer?
22. What has Sally got?
23. What was 20 pounds? How much were the trousers?
24. How many different stamps has he got?
25. Who did we see in Salzburg last week?
26. Who is Mum going to invite?

27. When did Peter win the downhill race in S.?
What did Peter win in Saalbach in 1997 ?
28. Whose brother is Tom?
29. What is Dad doing?
30. What is he fishing?
31. When did Mike and Ann go to the cinema?
32. What does mother never play?
33. What has Rick got?
34. Who said nothing to Tim?
Who did Brenda say nothing to?
35. Who usually goes to bed at eight?, When do our / your children usually go to bed?